KINGS AND PRIESTS UNTO GOD

Principles and Practice of
Spiritual Governance

Okey Onuzo

Kings and Priests Unto God: The Principles and

Practice of Spiritual Governance

Copyright © 2023, Okey Onuzo

ISBN: 978-1-880608-22-7

FIRST EDITION
Published by,
Life Link Worldwide Publishers,
175 Raymond Court Fayetteville GA.

For more information and book orders: amazon.com

TABLE OF CONTENTS

INTRODUCTION 1

CHAPTER 1: EMPOWERED TO REIGN 3

CHAPTER 2: SPIRITUAL EMPOWERMENT - THE ANOINTING 8

CHAPTER 3: AUTHORITY AND POWER...18

CHAPTER 4: MAN, MADE INFERIOR ONLY TO ELOHIM 29

CHAPTER 5: THE RESIDENTIAL KINGDOM 36

CHAPTER 6: SPIRITUAL GOVERNANCE..48

CHAPTER 7: SOVEREIGN GRACE — INDISPENSABLE
TO SPIRITUAL GOVERNANCE 64

CHAPTER 8: THE POWER OF THE REMNANT CHURCH.........................72

CHAPTER 9: SEPARATION, CONSECRATION,
AND SANCTIFICATION FOR 81

CHAPTER 10: KINGS AND PRIESTS AND IMPORTUNITY.......................87

CHAPTER 11: DIVINE CHARTER OF INCLUSION.................................98

CHAPTER 12: WALKING IN POWER 108

CHAPTER 13: PRACTICING SPIRITUAL GOVERNANCE.........................132

CHAPTER 14: ADDENDUM MARCHING ORDERS AND
GOVERNANCE PRAYERS..137

ACTUALIZING PA S.G. ELTON'S PROPHECY - THE MAKING OF A
RIGHTEOUS NIGERIA 141

INTRODUCTION

The best way to introduce this book is to say that it is a journey of discovery. It began on June 28, 1970, the day I gave my life to Christ. I made a commitment to follow Christ on that day, but it was not a total commitment. That was to come some 18 months later or thereabouts when I attended an odd-hour meeting of enthusiastic young believers in Christ at the Chapel of Resurrection of the University of Ibadan. I was a fledgling first-year pre-clinical medical student. I felt I qualified to attend the meeting even though I was still somewhat at the edge. Then Pastor Elton spoke to everybody and to nobody, but I knew he was speaking to me when he said: "Young man, let me tell you. You can never be better than God can make you." That was it. That was all I needed to hear to jump in with no holds barred.

Next was something from the Parable of the Sower: "Unto you, it is given to understand the mysteries of the Kingdom of God." "There must be mysteries waiting to be unlocked," I said to myself many times over. And why not, for there are mysteries everywhere in nature being discovered. After we discovered gravity, we discovered flight and other things like geostationary orbit and many more. Our

Lord Jesus said that it is the privilege of the believer to delve into the mysteries of the Kingdom of God.

Then our Lord Jesus said something to His disciples and would-be disciples that struck me: "You shall know the truth, and the truth shall make you free (John 8:32)." Somewhere deep in the spiritual realm must exist some liberating pieces of truth that enable a person to walk freely, while traveling this highway that leads from earth to heaven. There must be so much to find about life in the Spirit to empower a man to live the very life that God Almighty intended when He created man in His own image.

Striving to live life in the Spirit was no mean task. Everywhere you turned, there were challenges and traps here, there, and yonder. Then, I stumbled on the Scripture that said that after He washed us from our sins in His blood, He made us Kings and Priests unto His God. Wow! And what exactly does that mean? I am supposed to be a king and a priest unto God, and it's like everything, and everyone is climbing all over me. It did not make sense in my situation.

It took a while, and the pieces began to fall into place like a jigsaw puzzle. Then I realized that I had been a king and a priest for a while but had no clue what it was all about.

As we travel together in this book, I pray that you will arise like I did to become a spiritual governor, making decrees to establish the divine will and purpose daily in all your jurisdiction.

Okey Onuzo

CHAPTER 1

EMPOWERED
TO REIGN

Psalm 8:1-6 (TEV)

¹ O LORD, our Lord, your greatness is seen in all the world! Your praise reaches up to the heavens; ² it is sung by children and babies. You are safe and secure from all your enemies; you stop anyone who opposes you.

³ When I look at the sky, which you have made, at the moon and the stars, which you set in their places— ⁴ what are human beings, that you think of them; mere mortals, that you care for them?

⁵ Yet you made them inferior only to yourself; you crowned them with glory and honor. ⁶You appointed them rulers over everything you made; you placed them over all creation:

This message is for believers in our Lord and Savior, Jesus Christ, particularly those who feel helpless in the face of pervasive evil and those who feel obligated to do something about it because they are not part of it and fear that if they do nothing, they might be dragged into it. In other words, this is for believers who are not part of the problem but do not want to watch evil. They want to do something about it.

Yes, our Lord Jesus Christ died to make us kings and priests unto God our Father.

Revelation 1:5-6 (NKJV)

⁵ and from Jesus Christ, the faithful witness, the firstborn from the dead, and the ruler over the kings of the earth. To Him who loved us and washed us from our sins in His own blood, ⁶ and has made us kings and priests to His God and Father, to Him be glory and dominion forever and ever. Amen.

Part of our discipleship program should include an understanding of spiritual governance. Men and women who understand that you may not be able to carry an AK-47 rifle to shoot at evil, you might not be able to carry a placard and walk the streets, and you might not be able to join in the physical combats, but you can still do something about evil from where you are. Writing to the Corinthian Church, the Apostle Paul stated:

2 Corinthians 10:3-6 (NKJV)

³ For though we walk in the flesh, we do not war according to the flesh.
⁴ For the weapons of our warfare are not carnal but mighty in God for pulling down strongholds,
⁵ casting down arguments and every high thing that exalts itself against the knowledge of God, bringing every thought into captivity to the obedience of Christ,
⁶ and being ready to punish all disobedience when your obedience is fulfilled.

Have you wondered how a small band of largely unlettered disciples managed to spread the Gospel of Jesus Christ to all of the then-known world within a short space of 20 to 30 years after our Lord Jesus ascended to heaven?

The secret was that they deployed their spiritual armory and wrestled control from the kingdom of darkness to flood their world with the Light of the life of our Lord Jesus Christ. And that's what you and I must do; that's what spiritual governance is all about. When you see dominant evil in the natural, you go into the spiritual realm, disconnect it, and then wait for it to perish from the roots, as the Apostle Peter noted (Mark 11:20-21).

A gentleman gave us a testimony that illustrates this. He said he was going home from work in Atlanta, Georgia, and he saw a new restaurant. A sign hung before it read: NUDIST RESTAURANT. In other words, all the waiters are expected to be nude when you go to eat there. So, he said to himself, "In this place? No! No!"

He decided to drive around the restaurant for thirty minutes and cursed it. When he felt relief, he drove home. A month later, they shut down. This was because he understood spiritual governance. He understood that when you want to stop evil on the earth, you have to go up there in the spiritual realm and disconnect it.

Our Lord Jesus Christ demonstrated that in the cursing of the fig tree. When you read the story in Mark 11, you'd wonder, what was the point of cursing the fig tree? The Bible says that it was not the time of figs, so you really couldn't blame the fig tree for not having figs on it. But our Lord Jesus was trying to teach His disciples that they can bring things down with the sword of the Spirit, words.

So, He came to the fig tree and said, "Let no man eat fruit from ˅er again!" The Bible says the disciples heard it. The next day, ˅ere passing by, Peter was shocked and said, "Master, the fig tree You cursed has perished from the roots." Jesus said to them, "Have faith in God."

Words are powerful.

In John 6:63, He said to them, "The words I speak to you, they are spirit and life." He said the letter profits nothing, but when the word is quickened by the Holy Spirit, power is released and it brings about change.

It is important for me and you to understand how this works because that's what we are supposed to be about. The Roman Empire was run with the services of over 60 million slaves. However, the Apostle Paul wrote: 'Those of you who are slaves, do not rebel against your masters. Serve them with honesty and integrity. Don't rebel. Those of you who are their masters, treat them with decency because we are all slaves of one Master, Christ (Ephesians 6:5-9)."

But did you know that Christianity dismantled slavery in the Roman Empire without firing one shot? The power behind the truth in the Gospel is available to us, so we do not watch evil and say helplessly, 'What can we do?' I always make a point about the man who was called 'King of Potato Island.' You come to him and say, "Sir, there are so many thieves in Potato Island." Then, the king says, "That's how I see it, too! Everywhere you turn, thief, thief, in this my domain."

This king is sounding helpless!

However, when you learn that we have been made 'kings and priests,' it is so that you and I can govern. People are not made kings and priests so that they can watch things go bad like mere bystanders and spectators. Paul and Barnabas took the gospel to all of Europe and Asia Minor within two years because they preached the gospel of power.

Our Lord Jesus Christ Himself said, "Tarry ye in the city of Jerusalem until you are endued with power." They understood that you can bring about changes when you wield spiritual authority and power. Their results were more a product of what they did in the spiritual realm than in the natural realm.

Phillip went to Samaria and preached Christ, and the entire city rose to believe. He stopped by the Ethiopian Eunuch and preached Christ, and the man went home and established a Church that has been alive for nearly 2000 years.

These phenomenal successes were products of spiritual governance. They understood that we bring about changes from the spiritual to the natural. This is what we must embrace and imbibe, particularly in the face of pervasive evil, so that we can bring about change from the spiritual to the natural. Our Lord Jesus did not go to Calvary to raise spectators as His followers. No. He made us kings and priests unto His God and our Father so that we would take charge on heaven's behalf and so become God's true regents on the earth.

CHAPTER 2

SPIRITUAL EMPOWERMENT - THE ANOINTING

You cannot be spiritual and fight without empowerment. The anointing breaks the yoke. The anointing is neither a feeling nor a shaking.

I once visited a colleague's house and noticed that his wife had a plaster on her hand. So, I said, "Ah, madam, what happened?" She said, "The spirit carried me here, then there, and then all around, and I fell and got injured."

"What kind of spirit could that be, carrying her all about?" I knew it was not the Spirit of God because the Bible says in 1 Corinthians 14:32 that the spirit of the prophet is subject to the prophet. When you come into God's presence and ask for the anointing, He will give it to you in accordance with Mark 11:24. Simply believe that you have received it, and go and operate in it. Don't wait for feelings.

Isaiah 10:27

It shall come to pass in that day
That his burden will be taken away from your shoulder,
And his yoke from your neck,
And the yoke will be destroyed because of the anointing oil.

This is spiritual governance. Imagine if there were 1000 Christians in a city operating in spiritual governance and giving orders: orders that cooperate with heaven to change things on earth. Negative situations would change in a matter of months and weeks. The way spiritual governance works is that when you make the order, there's an interval. How do we know that? The devil goes to God and gets permission to attack Job.

Job 1:6-12 (KJV)

⁶Now, there was a day when the sons of God came to present themselves before the Lord, and Satan came also among them. ⁷And the Lord said unto Satan, Whence comest thou? Then Satan answered the Lord, and said, From going to and fro in the earth, and from walking up and down in it.
⁸And the Lord said unto Satan, Hast thou considered my servant Job, that there is none like him in the earth, a perfect and an upright man, one that feareth God, and escheweth evil? ⁹Then Satan answered the Lord, and said, Doth Job fear God for nought? ¹⁰Hast not thou made an hedge about him, and about his house, and about all that he hath on every side? thou hast blessed the work of his hands, and his substance is increased in the land.
¹¹But put forth thine hand now, and touch all that he hath, and he will curse thee to thy face. ¹²And the Lord said unto Satan, Behold, all that he hath is in thy power; only upon himself put not forth thine hand. So Satan went forth from the presence of the Lord.

Permission is everything. Once heaven grants the permission, that's it because nothing happens without God's permission. So, the devil went and got permission to attack Job's life. However, there was an interval between when he got the permission and when he attacked Job. Between the first day when the devil got permission and the day he attacked is what I call the window of opportunity. Those who are spiritually sensitive to discern that the devil is seeking permission to attack can intercept it through repentance and prayer. This is the message revealed to us in the Bible where it says that the saints overcame their accuser, the devil, by the blood of the Lamb (Revelation 12:10-11). Those who repent of their sins and forsake their old ways make it impossible for the devil to get permission over their lives. We are told that the blood of Jesus Christ cleanses us from *all* sin (1 John 1:7).

IMPERATIVES OF SPIRITUAL GOVERNANCE

You and I must know these things and bear them in mind if we want to exercise spiritual authority.

Understand Permission

Job1:12 (NIV)

12 The LORD said to Satan, "Very well, then, everything he has is in your power, but on the man himself do not lay a finger." Then Satan went out from the presence of the LORD.

The calamities that overtook Job's family and investments could not have happened without this permission. This is because there is only one center of power in the entire universe: God (Psalm 62:11).

Understand that We are Regents

First things first, we are regents who carry out orders. We don't institute orders. No, we carry out orders. We are not the King. Every permission must pass through the King. No one can do anything in God's world without His say, so. It is not possible. For the devil to attack Job, God had to permit him to do so. You and I need to get that. Every regent must grasp the revelation of Psalm 62:11 and 12. "More than once, I have heard God say that power belongs to Him."

Psalm 62:11-12 (NKJV)

[11]God has spoken once, Twice I have heard this: That power belongs to God. [12]Also to You, O Lord, belongs mercy; For You render to each one according to his work.

We must not listen to the people who think, "Oh, God and the devil are fighting." The Almighty God fights with no one. Absolutely not. Every creature must bow in submission by the law of creation, everywhere and anywhere the Creator is. Certain people think, "Oh, God and the devil are fighting, and it is such that the devil is winning sometimes." There's no such thing. Such a scenario cannot exist. Knowing this truth empowers us to govern confidently, knowing that whatever God says is final. For the devil to attack Job, he had to go to God and say to Him, 'You put a hedge around him. We can't cross it. However, if you move the hedge, we'll show the man what we can do." Then, God moved the hedge.

He put Job's business outside the hedge. He put Job's children outside the hedge, and only Job and his wife remained inside the hedge. It bears repeating that the day the devil got the permission was not the day he attacked Job. There was an interval that we call the 'Window of Opportunity.' This is the gap between the permission and the action. When we understand how the system works, we must know that those who desire preventive living must learn how to stop the devil from getting that all-important permission. How do we do that?

Preventing Permission

The Bible tells us in the Book of Revelation that the devil is the accuser of the brethren. The purpose of the accusation is to stop believers from being empowered when they come into God's presence. Holiness is the foundation of power; therefore, never listen to anyone who ridicules holiness because no man can see God without it. Righteousness is the foundation of God's throne. The reason why no being can match God's power is because no being can match His holiness. "God is Light, and in Him, there is no darkness at all." (1 John 1:5)

So, when the devil comes before God to get permission to attack a saint, what is he using? He is using all those things you and I are doing that offend God. Therefore, anyone who understands governance, will not allow devils to get permission over his life. We learn to be careful with words so we don't ensnare ourselves by the words of our mouth (Proverbs 6:2). We learn to say only words that edify, words that are seasoned with salt.

Ephesians 4:29 (NKJV)

29Let no unwholesome word proceed from your mouth, but only such a word as is good for edification according to the need of the moment, so that it will give grace to those who hear.

12

Colossians 4:6 (NKJV)

⁶Let your speech always be with grace, seasoned with salt, that you may know how you ought to answer each one.

The devil can't get permission with those ones. Do you know why he cannot get it?

Psalm145:17 (NKJV)

¹⁷The Lord is righteous in all His ways, Gracious in all His works.

In other words, God cannot grant the devil permission, and then someone will go before Him and say, 'You were unfair to me.' No. God is righteous in all His ways. He cannot grant unfair permissions. So, it's important for us to understand governance so that we don't talk, live, and behave anyhow. If we do, it will hurt us before God unless we repent.

Never forget that those who persist in doing evil empower the enemy to get permission over their lives. When we are alive to the way the spiritual works, we are careful about what we say and do because we know that the enemy is waiting to go and get permission. The Bible says in that scripture **Psalm 62:12 (NKJV):**

¹²Also to You, O Lord, belongs mercy; For You render to each one according to his work.

Here is another imperative of governance.

Repentance will Block Permission

God's love is constant. He rewards everyone according to their deeds. They can't get permission without us doing something or saying something wrong or evil. That's why the Father gave us the

Blood of Jesus to wash our sins away. What did the Bible say? If we walk in the light as He is in the light, the Blood of Jesus Christ will cleanse us from all sins (1 John 1:7).

Suppose someone says or does something wrong. The devil will run to heaven to accuse him before the Father. As we have said, iniquity gives the enemy ammunition to get permission. Yes, he gets ammunition with sin. That's why we must understand repentance as an important part of spiritual governance.

Repentance is not apologizing and going back to the sin. Have you heard of those people whose idea of repentance is to say 'sorry,' but tomorrow they will still do the same thing again? That's not how it works because the devil will still get permission when we do it that way. After we have said sorry from the heart, we must commit to change. That's what genuine repentance is about. Attacks don't just happen because God does not give permission anyhow. The Bible says we must not be ignorant of the tricks of the devil (2 Corinthians 2:11). When we display such spiritual ignorance, it can only empower the enemy and hurt us in the end. This is a type of the universal and eternal Law of sowing and reaping. We may sow and forget. But the enemy does not forget. That is why we are often surprised when an attack penetrates our shield. And then we are heard to ask, 'But what did I do?' So, it's important to understand the way the spiritual system runs.

Genesis 15:12-16 NKJV

12 Now when the sun was going down, a deep sleep fell upon Abram; and behold, horror and great darkness fell upon him. 13 Then He said to Abram: "Know certainly that your descendants will be strangers in a land that is not theirs, and will serve them, and they will afflict them four hundred years. 14 And also the *nation whom they serve I will judge; afterward they shall come out with great possessions. ¹⁵ Now as for you, you shall [d]go to your fathers in peace; you shall be buried at a good old age. ¹⁶ But in the fourth generation they shall return here, for the iniquity of the Amorites is not yet complete."*

It is possible to read and not understand the significance of these verses. The LORD was saying to Abraham, "I'm a God of justice and righteousness, and I am going to dispossess the Amorites and give your descendants this land as an inheritance. But Abram, hear Me, they will have to complete the full measure of their iniquity, and I'm telling you, it may take about 400 years. These Amorites are sinning very slowly, so their cup of iniquity will take 400 years to fill up." Now, somebody ignorant of the way of the LORD may come and hear this prophecy and exclaim, "400 years? No. The most they should have is 20 years because I am in a hurry to take possession. They may then begin to fast and pray for them to be dispossessed quickly. "Oh God of all heaven and earth, I ask that these Amorites be dispossessed quickly."

Will such a prayer be answered under the circumstances? The answer is No; it cannot be answered. But why can't it be answered? It is because God is righteous in all His ways. He cannot dispossess the Amorites before their cup of iniquity is full. But you know, nobody can go to God and suggest: 'Why can't the people sin faster? You know, LORD, I want to possess my inheritance quickly. Is that a prayer God can answer? Certainly not, for God is righteous in all His ways. Anytime it appears that God is unfair, then know that we lack the full information of what has transpired. The outcome of this Amorite story is that it took 430 years for them to be dispossessed.

The other reason, of course, is that it took 400 years for Abraham to go from a family to a nation.

No matter how much in a hurry you are, you cannot hurry this kind of situation. That's what the Bible says in Psalm 75: that promotion does not come from the East or from the West. It says, 'God is the judge. He brings down one, and He lifts up another.' The man you want to replace is sinning slowly, you know. It is, therefore, impossible to replace him now. His cup of iniquity must fill up before judgment can overtake him, for God is righteous in all His ways.

We need to understand these things about spiritual governance. We don't make decisions; we receive them, so no matter how we exercise our spiritual authority, we must always remember that God is righteous in all His ways and so does not permit injustice. It's important to understand that.

The Amorites' iniquity is not completed, so there's no way to uproot them before 400 years are over. No spiritual governor can change that, no matter how close to God, because of the power of that scripture that says that God is righteous in all His ways.

Additionally, in 1 John 1:5, we are told there is no iniquity or injustice in God. "This is the message we heard from our Lord Jesus and now declare to you: 'God is light, and there is no darkness in Him at all.'" Yes! There is no evil in God, no injustice. God is never unfair.

Part of our problem is that we don't have all the information for any given situation. As a result, we may find ourselves in a situation and think God is unfair. This only appears so because we lack information.

There are so many Scriptures that confirm this. Here is a story in the Bible. The wife of Jeroboam, the first King of the Northern

Kingdom of Israel, went to Ahijah, the prophet, to ask about her son, who was sick (1 Kings 14). She disguised herself. The prophet said, "Remove your veil, for I have already seen you. That boy is going to die. But do you know why? He's the only righteous person in your family, so he'll get a decent funeral. For the rest of you, dogs will eat you up."

God is righteous in all His ways and comprehensive in everything that He does. That's what God is like. In Him, there's no darkness at all. So, we cannot decree something that is out of sync with God's timing and expect it to happen. It will not happen because of the nature of God and because God is in control of everything. So, we can speak of maturing decrees waiting for the fullness of time. Israel waited in Egypt for 430 years before they could enter their inheritance.

CHAPTER 3

AUTHORITY
AND POWER

God wants us to enjoy our power and authority in Christ.

Revelation 5:1-6 (NKJV)

¹And I saw in the right hand of Him who sat on the throne a scroll written inside and on the back, sealed with seven seals. ²Then I saw a strong angel proclaiming with a loud voice, "Who is worthy to open the scroll and to loose its seals?" ³And no one in heaven or on the earth or under the earth was able to open the scroll, or to look at it.

⁴So I wept much, because no one was found worthy to open and read the scroll, or to look at it. ⁵ But one of the elders said to me, "Do not weep. Behold, the Lion of the tribe of Judah, the Root of David, has prevailed to open the scroll and to loose its seven seals."

The picture that emerges in these verses reveals the truth of what we have studied already about the awesome power of holiness before God and obedience to His will on the earth. The scroll contains the decrees of Almighty God about the final destiny of both obedient and disobedient humanity. But who can unseal the scroll, and what is the qualification?

First, we look at the complete list of the unqualified in **Revelation 5:2-3 (NKJV)"**

²Then I saw a strong angel proclaiming with a loud voice, "Who is worthy to open the scroll and to loose its seals?" ³And no one in heaven or on the earth or under the earth was able to open the scroll or to look at it.

First, no one in heaven was found among the triumphant saints, angels, and archangels. Second, no one on earth was found among the Saints militant on the earth like you and me. Third, no one under the earth was found. This would be among the disembodied spirits and devils.

No one was found because no one had the holiness, purity, and complete obedience that would qualify them to open this book of decrees and judgment. The reason for this is that to open it, nothing must be written there concerning any misdeed of the person. This is the revelation of **John 8:46 (NKJV):**

⁴⁶Which of you convicts Me of sin? And if I tell the truth, why do you not believe Me?

This is corroborated by **Hebrews 4:15 (NKJV):**

¹⁵For we do not have a High Priest who cannot sympathize with our weaknesses but was in all points tempted as we are, yet without sin.

I want us to pay attention to **Revelation 5: 5.**

But one of the elders said to me, "Do not weep. Behold, the Lion of the tribe of Judah, the Root of David, has prevailed to open the scroll and to loose its seven seals."

Our Lord Jesus Christ prevailed over the world, the flesh, and the devil while He was here on His mission to the world. In His three temptations in the wilderness, He triumphed over the lusts of the flesh, the lusts of the eyes, and the pride of life. As a result of this, the Lord God Almighty gave Him a name above every name, that at the name of Jesus, every knee must bow in heaven and on earth and every tongue must confess that Jesus Christ is Lord, to the glory of the Father.

Through this, we see the purpose of our Lord Jesus Christ in making us kings and priests unto God, which is to raise a people on earth who will be citizens of heaven passing through the earth.

Philippians 3:20-21 (NKJV)

20 For our citizenship is in heaven, from which we also eagerly wait for the Savior, the Lord Jesus Christ, 21 who will transform our lowly body that it may be conformed to His glorious body, according to the working by which He is able even to subdue all things to Himself.

As citizens of heaven passing through the earth, we constantly appear before the God of heaven to worship with the angels and archangels and to be empowered like the angels to do God's will on earth as it is done in heaven.

Kings and priests are God's regents on earth to cause the purposes of God Almighty to be established on the earth. We do this by making decrees establishing God's Kingdom and will on the earth.

Job 22:28-30 (KJV)

28Thou shalt also decree a thing, and it shall be established unto thee: and the light shall shine upon thy ways. 29When men are cast down, then thou shalt say, There is lifting up; and he shall save the humble person. 30He shall deliver the island of the innocent: and it is delivered by the pureness of thine hands.

As priests, we enter God's presence to receive the decree we should make and how we should make it. We come forth to make the decrees as directed.

I recall once when my city had a real menace of robbers. The Holy Spirit revealed that I should curse every income earned through robbery and violence. After about two weeks of that, the military head of state reshuffled state governors. The new governor sent to us introduced sweeping measures that curbed the menace. It became clear that when we do as we are told, heaven will respond with the solution to the problem. Therefore, because we are priests in the order of Melchizedek, our decrees must also be in the order of Melchizedek as revealed to us in **Hebrews 7:1-3 (KJV):**

1For this Melchisedec, king of Salem, priest of the most high God, who met Abraham returning from the slaughter of the kings, and blessed him; 2To whom also Abraham gave a tenth part of all; first being by interpretation King of righteousness, and after that also King of Salem, which is, King of peace; 3Without father, without mother, without descent, having neither beginning of days, nor end of life; but made like unto the Son of God; abideth a priest continually.

- First, King of Righteousness
- Second, King of Peace

King of Righteousness

The general meaning of righteousness is conformity to a standard. There is also a connotation of justice. The most consistent element in the pursuit of righteousness is the will and the intention to do the right thing, get it right, and get things moving in the right direction. This raises the question of how to determine what is right. The Pharisees externalized righteousness and were condemned by our Lord Jesus in **Matthew 23:23-24 (KJV):**

23 Woe unto you, scribes and Pharisees, hypocrites! for ye pay tithe of mint and anise and cummin, and have omitted the weightier matters of the law, judgment, mercy, and faith: these ought ye to have done, and not to leave the other undone. 24 Ye blind guides, which strain at a gnat, and swallow a camel.

Early Hebrew thought associated righteousness with conformity with the commandments of God, as we are told in **Deuteronomy 6:24-25 (NKJV):**

24 And the LORD commanded us to observe all these statutes, to fear the LORD our God, for our good always, that He might preserve us alive, as it is this day. 25 Then it will be righteousness for us, if we are careful to observe all these commandments before the LORD our God, as He has commanded us.'

These commandments aim to improve the quality of the human character for the good of all. Controlling that improvement is the fear of God, who gave the commandment and punishes disobedience and blesses obedience. This is clearly seen in the Ten Commandments and its two strands of the commandment to love. First is the love for God, and next is the love for our neighbor in obedience to God.

Abraham had a notion of the righteousness of God, which powered his intercession for Sodom in **Genesis 18:25 (NKJV):**

25 Far be it from You to do such a thing as this, to slay the righteous with the wicked, so that the righteous should be as the wicked; far be it from You! Shall not the Judge of all the earth do right?"

When the prophet Isaiah spoke about the vicarious death of our Lord Jesus Christ, he revealed that God's righteousness has both morality and self-sacrificing love.

Isaiah 53:4-6 (NKJV)

4 Surely He has borne our griefs and carried our sorrows; Yet we esteemed Him stricken, Smitten by God, and afflicted. 5 But He was wounded for our transgressions, He was bruised for our iniquities; The chastisement for our peace was upon Him, And by His stripes we are healed. 6 All we like sheep have gone astray; We have turned, everyone, to his own way; And the LORD has laid on Him the iniquity of us all.

This was a revelation of how far the God of righteousness is willing to go to raise the quality of the human character so that it can aspire to resemble that of God who created us. No wonder we are told in **Romans 8:29-30 (NKJV):**

29 For whom He foreknew, He also predestined to be conformed to the image of His Son, that He might be the firstborn among many brethren. 30 Moreover whom He predestined, these He also called; whom He called, these He also justified; and whom He justified, these He also glorified.

As kings of righteousness, we must aim at the continuous improvement of the human character that must portray and reveal the character of the God of righteousness. This will include love, justice, equity, truth, and compassion. It is for the same reason that we never support or endorse evil, for that will be contrary to the nature and character of the God of righteousness, as revealed in **Psalm 145:17 (KJV):**

¹⁷The LORD is righteous in all His ways and holy in all His works.

Some years ago, a lady told a story in a place where I preached this message. In her office, some young men were collecting bribes. When she challenged them, they retorted that their bosses were receiving bribes in their offices, so they would do the same.

One day, she got incensed in her soul and said to God, "How can I be here and this will be happening? I command it, stop!" Two weeks later, her colleagues demanded a bribe from a certain lady, and unknown to them, she was the sister of their boss. That was how the whole thing stopped. You and I need to understand spiritual authority.

I was in London a while ago, and we have been praying against the LGBTQ plus agenda and the confusion it was bringing to the understanding and practice of Bible-based morality, holiness, righteousness, and truth. One of our requests to the Lord was that all who repent should become ministers and evangelists of the Truth according to the Gospel to those who are still in the movement. When I mentioned this, a man spoke up in excitement, "Oh yes, yes. It is happening in my neighborhood. They are gathering them together and ministering to them."

I realized that we may never know to what extent our exercise of spiritual authority is impacting our world. We may never know where and how the Lord is deploying our exercise of spiritual authority for good and for God in the world. What matters is that we are not spectators observing change or the lack of it in our world. Instead, in our little corners, we are impacting our world on our knees through the exercise of spiritual governance. This is very practical; any believer in our Lord Jesus Christ can engage in it.

King of Peace

Melchizedek was the King of Peace. The Kingdom of God is righteousness, peace, and joy in the Holy Ghost. It is our duty to pursue peace in all our ways and all our conduct. We are told that peace and holiness go together in **Hebrews 12:14 (NKJV)**:

14Pursue peace with all people, and holiness, without which no one will see the Lord:

Our Lord Jesus taught us that peacemakers are children of God.

Matthew 5:9 (NKJV)

9 Blessed are the peacemakers, For they shall be called sons of God.

There are three dimensions of this peace.

- The first is peace with God.

Romans 5:1 (NKJV)

1Therefore, having been justified by faith, we have peace with God through our Lord Jesus Christ.

- The second is peace with our neighbor.

Romans 12:18 (NKJV)

18 If it is possible, as much as depends on you, live peaceably with all men.

We are told that it is a product of a life that has been seasoned by the life of Christ.

Mark 9:50 (NKJV)

50 Salt is good, but if the salt loses its flavor, how will you season it? Have salt in yourselves, and have peace with one another."

- The third is peace within ourselves, which is a product of our faith in God.

Philippians 4:4-7 (NKJV)

4Rejoice in the Lord always. Again, I will say, rejoice! 5Let your gentleness be known to all men. The Lord is at hand. 6Be anxious for nothing, but in everything by prayer and supplication, with thanksgiving, let your requests be made known to God; 7and the peace of God, which surpasses all understanding, will guard your hearts and minds through Christ Jesus.

But what is the enemy's strategy? It is to preoccupy us with what we can eat, where we will live, what dresses we will wear, and what cars and private jets we will ride. While we are busy with all that, the enemy is totally unchallenged in the spirit realm, and so is able to superintend pervasive evil all around us.

Let's say you are praying earnestly and dismantling things in the spirit when, suddenly, your driver bashes your car. Then, you jettison your governance prayers, and now, distracted, all you talk about is your car. There are many distractions, but you and I must recognize the enemy at work through these distractions and refuse to be diverted. We must identify the distractions, deal with them, and refocus on our spiritual governance duties.

That was why our Lord Jesus told His disciples in **Matthew 6:31-34 (NKJV):**

³¹ Therefore, do not worry, saying, 'What shall we eat?' or 'What shall we drink?' or 'What shall we wear?' ³² For after all these things the Gentiles seek. For your heavenly Father knows that you need all these things. ³³But seek first the kingdom of God and His righteousness, and all these things shall be added to you. ³⁴Therefore do not worry about tomorrow, for tomorrow will worry about its own things. Sufficient for the day is its own trouble.

That's why He gave that assurance: If we focus on getting the Kingdom of God to reside in the hearts and lives of men, He will meet our needs. Today, everywhere you turn, evil is being promoted. They are calling evil good and good evil. To take back our world and restore the Kingdom of God and its righteousness, we must understand and practice spiritual governance so we can bring about changes in our world from the spiritual to the natural.

Man's Hierarchy in Creation

This is the first thing to note in the practice of spiritual governance. I call this *creational hierarchy*. The LORD God Almighty made man inferior only to Himself. Why is that important to note?

It is because there are many in Christ who are still afraid of devils and his agents. They feel threatened if someone were to suggest that if they persist in trying to stop what they consider profitable evil, they would contact devils to stop them. Here in Nigeria, they may say something like, "I will go to the riverside to deal with you." If we go away scared by such a threat, part of the reason must be that we are ignorant of man's hierarchy in creation. We are made inferior only to God and so must rise to become who we were meant to be. If we know that we are made inferior only to God, no threat from devils should make our hearts miss a beat. This is the power of the knowledge of the truth which our Lord Jesus taught in

John 8:31-32 (NKJV)

31 Then Jesus said to those Jews who believed Him, "If you abide in My word, you are My disciples indeed. 32 And you shall know the truth, and the truth shall make you free."

Let us note that humans do not have spiritual power, only authority, and we are made inferior only to God. That's awesome if we understand it and walk boldly in it through faith. This means that no devil is higher than us in creation. That's why the Scripture says in 1 John 4:4 that you have overcome them because greater is He that is in you than he that is in the world.

After we are born again, the Holy Spirit of God comes to indwell us to empower us and the decrees we make in the exercise of our spiritual authority in governance. Whatever decrees devils make through men are effectively countered by the decrees made by saints of God and of Christ who are empowered by the Holy Spirit of God. That is the meaning of 1 John 4:4: "You have overcome them because greater is He that is in you than he that is in the world."

This is the truth that makes us free. It empowers the previously oppressed to break free and begin to exercise spiritual authority in governance to the glory of God.

CHAPTER 4

MAN, MADE INFERIOR ONLY TO ELOHIM

Psalm 8:3-5 TEV

³When I look at the sky, which you have made, at the moon and the stars, which you set in their places— ⁴ what are human beings, that you think of them; mere mortals, that you care for them? ⁵ Yet you made them inferior only to yourself; you crowned them with glory and honor.

The revelation in this passage is mind-boggling, and that is why we are revisiting it. The Almighty is ever thinking about us because He made us a little lower than Himself so we can rule the world He gave us by being one with Him in purpose and action.

The statement that we were made inferior to God only speaks of where God positioned us at creation. Man is higher in the hierarchy of creation than all angels. It does not appear so to many because God gave man authority, but He gave the angels power.

But listen to our Lord Jesus Christ in **Luke 10:17-20 (NKJV):**

[17]Then the seventy returned with joy, saying, "Lord, even the demons are subject to us in Your name." [18] And He said to them, "I saw Satan fall like lightning from heaven. [19]Behold, I give you the authority to trample on serpents and scorpions, and over all the power of the enemy, and nothing shall by any means hurt you. [20]Nevertheless, do not rejoice in this, that the spirits are subject to you, but rather rejoice because your names are written in heaven."

Here, the Lord gives us the charter of invincibility – nothing can harm you, irrespective of what the enemy uses. The authority we have is sufficient for us to deal with all, not some, but all the powers of the enemy. The reason is that our authority is backed by the power of God and His Christ, which is the awesome comprehensive power of the Holy Spirit. Witches and those in the occult are humans, and so have no power. They must consult devils to use power. This is the meaning of the message of

1 John 4:4 (NKJV):

[4]You are of God, little children, and have overcome them, because He who is in you is greater than he who is in the world.

The Holy Spirit that indwells the believer is far greater in power than the quantum of power given to any and every angel. When the scriptures say that power is exclusive to God, it refers to the power revealed by the Holy Spirit.

That is why the scripture reads: "What is man that you are mindful of him? You have made him a little lower than Elohim." Apostle Paul wrote in 1 Corinthians 6:3: "Don't you know that we shall judge angels?" Because man is higher in the hierarchy of creation, the Bible affirms that we shall judge angels. So, it is important to understand who you are and who God has made you in Christ Jesus. This is the first rule in spiritual governance.

There are three questions before us:

- "How many people that go to Church know this?"
- The other question is, "How many people that go to Church believe this?"
- And finally, "How many people that go to Church receive this and walk daily in the experience of spiritual governance as a result of it?"

When we understand spiritual governance, we know who we are and what we have. Empowered by that truth, we can step forward to cause the will and purposes of God to be done on the earth in our lives and world.

Luke 24:49 (NKJV)

⁴⁹Behold, I send the Promise of My Father upon you; but tarry in the city of Jerusalem until you are endued with power from on high."

We are empowered in His presence while we worship by faith with the angels, the four living creatures, and the saints triumphant, represented by the 24 elders. Our Lord Jesus Christ taught empowerment through faith in **Mark 11:22-24 (NRSV)**.

²²Jesus answered them, "Have faith in God. ²³Truly I tell you, if you say to this mountain, 'Be taken up and thrown into the sea,' and if you do not doubt in your heart, but believe that what you say will come to pass, it will be done for you. ²⁴So I tell you, whatever you ask for in prayer, believe that you have received it, and it will be yours.

This scripture holds the secret to empowerment. We must connect to God's will, the Kingdom of God and its righteousness, and godliness and righteousness in our lives and our world, always remembering that it is not about us but about the glory of God in us and through us.

Remember that the fourfold glory will emerge when we get it right like our Lord Jesus taught us.

John 13:31-32 (NRSV):

31When he (Judas) had gone out, Jesus said, "Now the Son of Man has been glorified, and God has been glorified in him. 32If God has been glorified in him, God will also glorify him in himself and will glorify him at once.

- The Son of Man is glorified through submitting to the divine will, which for our Lord Jesus here was death on the Cross.
- God is glorified in Him, which means the glory that God receives through our salvation is guaranteed by the obedience of Christ.
- God will glorify the Son of Man in Himself, is revealed in the Scripture that says, "for God so loved the world that He gave His only begotten Son, that whoever believes in Him, will not perish but have everlasting life (John 3:16). This is how God is glorifying the Son of Man in Himself. We also see this in

1 John 4:9-10 (NRSV):

⁹God's love was revealed among us in this way: God sent his only Son into the world so that we might live through him. ¹⁰In this is love, not that we loved God but that he loved us and sent his Son to be the atoning sacrifice for our sins.

- God will glorify the Son of Man at once. This glory was revealed through the resurrection of our Lord Jesus Christ from the dead. The glory of the Father and the Son are intertwined, so it will happen at once. The glory was revealed in this reassuring conversation with the Father:

John 12:27-28 (TEV)

²⁷ "Now my heart is troubled—and what shall I say? Shall I say, 'Father, do not let this hour come upon me'? But that is why I came—so that I might go through this hour of suffering. ²⁸ Father, bring glory to your name!" Then a voice spoke from heaven, "I have brought glory to it, and I will do so again."

And this glory was seen a few days later at the resurrection.

We, therefore, seek empowerment so that the Father may be glorified in His Son as revealed to us in **John 14:12-13 (NKJV):**

¹²"Most assuredly, I say to you, he who believes in Me, the works that I do he will do also; and greater works than these he will do, because I go to My Father. ¹³And whatever you ask in My name, that I will do, that the Father may be glorified in the Son.

We are made priests of the Most High God in Christ and through Christ. Through the sacrifice of Christ, we are made holy, pure, and faultless before God (Colossians 1:21-22). This means there is not a single thing you can put to our charge before God because we have been made holy by the Blood of Jesus.

The Blood of Jesus – The Way into His Presence

The Blood of Jesus makes a man worthy to come into the presence of the Most Holy God, to be empowered. We have a Father who is more eager to answer than we are ready to pray.

Hebrews 10:19-22 (NLT2)

19 And so, dear brothers and sisters, we can boldly enter heaven's Most Holy Place because of the Blood of Jesus. 20 By his death, Jesus opened a new and life-giving way through the curtain into the Most Holy Place. 21 And since we have a great High Priest who rules over God's house, 22 let us go right into the presence of God with sincere hearts fully trusting him. For our guilty consciences have been sprinkled with Christ's blood to make us clean, and our bodies have been washed with pure water.

Entering into God's Most Holy presence in heaven through the Blood of Jesus must be routine for us. Saints who are militant on earth can only appear before God for empowerment through the Blood of Jesus.

Our Lord Jesus summarized our lives as kings and priests unto God when He taught us to pray in **Matthew 6:9-10 (NKJV):**

9 In this manner, therefore, pray: Our Father in heaven, Hallowed be Your name. 10 Your kingdom come. Your will be done on earth as it is in heaven.

Kings and priests unto God are empowered to establish the Kingdom of God in the hearts of men and women on earth.

Luke 17:20-21 (NKJV):

[20]Now when He was asked by the Pharisees when the kingdom of God would come, He answered them and said, "The kingdom of God does not come with observation; [21]nor will they say, 'See here!' or 'See there!' For indeed, the kingdom of God is within you."

Kings and priests unto God, in their pursuit of righteousness and peace on the earth, are to do the will of God on earth as it is in heaven. And this is achieved as we are led by the Holy Spirit in all things. To be led by the Holy Spirit, we must maintain communion with Him as we are told in the prayer seen in **2 Corinthians 13:14:** *"The grace of our Lord Jesus Christ, the love of God and **the communion of the Holy Spirit** be with you all."* The communion of the Holy Spirit is basic for spiritual life, particularly so for kings and priests unto God.

CHAPTER 5

THE RESIDENTIAL KINGDOM

Luke 17:20-21 (NKJV)

²⁰Now when He was asked by the Pharisees when the kingdom of God would come, He answered them and said, "The kingdom of God does not come with observation; ²¹nor will they say, 'See here!' or 'See there!' For indeed, the kingdom of God is within you."

As kings and priests unto God, our primary duty is to establish the Kingdom of God in the lives of men and women in our world so that we can all rise to live the Christ-life in the world. When the Kingdom of God is resident in us, it will bring forth righteousness, peace, and joy in the Holy Ghost through our lives to impact our world.

Our Lord Jesus explained to His disciples that the Holy Spirit has to come for logistical reasons. He needs to be with each of them in different locations at the same time. His purpose is to establish the

Kingdom of God and its righteousness in us first so we can become Light in a world of darkness.

He is the Teacher in that School of Discipleship made of one student, you or me. We are called to cultivate companionship so we can have His help and counsel in all situations.

It is important to note that the Holy Spirit can be grieved. And when He is grieved, He may leave us. As the experience of Samson, in the Book of Judges reveals, we may not be aware that He has left. Without the presence of the Holy Spirit in us, the power to establish the Kingdom of God in the lives of men with conviction and conversion is cut off. This is the message of **Ephesians 3:20-21 (NKJV)**

[20] Now to Him who is able to do exceedingly abundantly above all that we ask or think, according to the power that works in us, [21] to Him be glory in the church by Christ Jesus to all generations, forever and ever. Amen.

The Holy Spirit is this source of power that works within us. His purpose is to control and direct us so that the Kingdom of God will prosper in us and through us.

The Holy Spirit is the power behind our authority. When we speak with authority wielding the Sword of the Spirit in our mouths, the Holy Spirit quickens the words we speak and empowers them to fulfill God's counsel in us and through us on earth.

You will recall that we have said that God gave the angels *dunamis,* from which we derive the word dynamite. But He gave man *exousia,* which is authority. Authority without power is meaningless. This is why the residential Holy Spirit is the power behind our authority. The Holy Spirit is far superior to any other power. He is the third person in the Trinity. This is why kings and priests unto God can exercise authority over every other power on the earth.

In my early days as a fledgling preacher, while still an undergraduate at the University of Ibadan, I went on a school visit and challenged the students to divest themselves of all "powerless powers," as we used to call them. Two boys ran back to their hostels and brought rings they said their fathers had given them for protection. Then, most preachers would advise that we burn the charms, but I had nothing to burn them with, so I simply threw them away and prayed for the students. I noticed pain in my left hand after returning to my university room.

I prayed, "Lord, have mercy!" And the enemy whispered to me, "Do you think everybody can throw such things away? No, only big preachers throw charms away!"

I didn't know how to counter that at the time, so I entertained such thoughts. This is why we must understand spiritual governance and the knowledge base required to conduct it effectively. I thought you had to be big to be able to do it. Later, I was properly instructed that those voices were testing my knowledge base. "Son, you have the authority, so stand on it and see what the LORD will do." That was communion from the Holy Spirit.

Subsequently, one of the university professors called us, three undergraduates, to say that his wife had juju in the house and that we should come and help him destroy them. So, we went there. When we got to their house, there was a calabash, a tortoise, and several of those things given by Juju men, ostensibly for protection. We brought them all out and set them on fire.

When I got to my room, it was like all the demons in Ibadan had come there to harass me. They were making noises in my ears. So, I knelt down and declared, "You demons here, I am going to sleep now. If I hear 'fim' from any of you, you'll go to hell prematurely..." It was as bold as I could get. That order spelled the end of all the noises.

I was able to stand on my authority because I had gained more knowledge. I was more informed about what it meant to be a king and a priest unto God through Christ. As the Bible reveals, I have become enlightened by the revelation of Christ. I had tasted of the heavenly gift of eternal life through Christ; I had become a partaker of the Holy Spirit, and more importantly, have tasted the good word of God and the powers of the age to come (Heb. 6:4-5). I went to bed that night and slept very soundly. It was a vital lesson on testing the powers we have received through Christ from our Father in heaven.

I got to know while visiting a Church some time ago that there are a few people who, out of desperation, seek solutions to their situations from native doctors and mediums. It is important to note that those who do that provoke the anger and jealousy of a Holy God. The Ten Commandments teach us clearly that the God we serve does not compete. He is too jealous to compete for our loyalty. Loyalty is critical in spiritual relationships. Here is what the LORD said to Moses in **Exodus 34:12-14 (NKJV)**

¹² Take heed to yourself, lest you make a covenant with the inhabitants of the land where you are going, lest it be a snare in your midst. ¹³ But you shall destroy their altars, break their sacred pillars, and cut down their wooden images ¹⁴ (for you shall worship no other god, for the LORD, whose name is Jealous, is a jealous God).

Such a disloyalty to the God who has called us will put us in mortal danger.

The power of God released on us is sufficient to deal with every assault of the enemy. This is the message of **Ephesians 1:19-22 (NLT2)**

[19] I also pray that you will understand the incredible greatness of God's power for us who believe him. This is the same mighty power [20] that raised Christ from the dead and seated him in the place of honor at God's right hand in the heavenly realms. [21] Now he is far above any ruler or authority or power or leader or anything else—not only in this world but also in the world to come. [22] God has put all things under the authority of Christ and has made him head over all things for the benefit of the church.

A new Creation in Christ

This is powerfully revealed in **2 Corinthians 5:17 NKJV**

Therefore, if anyone is in Christ, he is a new creation; old things have passed away; behold, all things have become new.

It is our duty to discover the life and authority of this new creation in Christ because it holds the key to our victories in spiritual engagement with the enemy. Those who know the truth can figuratively stamp their foot on the ground and insist that old things must pass away. Through faith in God, we bring down the divine presence in our lives, and the anointing will break any and every yoke of bondage. So, we must be determined to get rid of our ignorance of spiritual truth, for knowledge brings faith, and faith brings down the presence and power of God.

This is why we must not submit to that deception and lie that says that a new creature in Christ can still be enslaved by devils. The solution to such an impasse is the knowledge of the truth that sets free (John 8:32). Let us hold firmly to the truth that our old nature with all spiritual entanglements and curses have passed away the day we gave our lives to Christ, which is also the day we moved from the kingdom of darkness to the Kingdom of Light. All of heaven will stand with us when we stand on this truth.

That is what our Lord Jesus was teaching His disciples in Mark 11. If you can believe, the truth you believe will work for you. "All things are possible to them that believe (Mark 9:23).

This is the Word of God revealed to us in Christ Jesus, that anyone who has come to God through Christ is a king and a priest unto God (Rev. 1:5 & 6).

Kings and Priests and God's Power

One truth revealed in the Bible is that Jesus' death and resurrection are not about religion but about power. This is why we teach that the power that brought our Lord Jesus back to life is available to kings and priests unto God (Ephesians 1:19-22).

Many years ago, my son fell into the soak-away pit. He developed a fever subsequently. My wife and I are doctors. We administered antibiotics, but his temperature remained very high, as high as 40^{0}C. I thought to myself, "What type of devil is this?" Then, one night, my wife said to me, "This boy's temperature has gone very high again!" That was when it dawned on me that a different kind of solution was needed. I carried the boy to the sitting room and declared over his body, "Devil, get out now!" That was it. His body temperature normalized immediately and never rose again.

The believer has the power to become a king and a priest unto God, so you and I must not elect to be spectators who allow the enemy to wreak havoc on our lives and in our world. It's about time we rose to become all our God has called us to be.

The Priesthood of the Saints

To understand our role as kings and priests unto our God, we must begin with the priesthood because the priesthood is the path to power.

What exactly does it mean to be a priest unto God?

When the priests minister in the temple in the Old Testament, they must first cleanse themselves from their sins before entering God's presence to commune with Him. In the Old Testament, the high priest ministering to God at the inner altar would have a bell or bells tied to their feet. For as long as the bell jingled, the other priests would know that all was well and the minister was alive in the presence of God. If the jingle stopped, they would pull him out with a rope previously attached to his leg.

When he came out of God's presence, the priest would give the people God's message that he received in His presence. We see this clearly from **Exodus 19:3-8 (NLT2)**:

3 Then Moses climbed the mountain to appear before God. The LORD called to him from the mountain and said, "Give these instructions to the family of Jacob; announce it to the descendants of Israel:

4 'You have seen what I did to the Egyptians. You know how I carried you on eagles' wings and brought you to myself.

5 Now if you will obey me and keep my covenant, you will be my own special treasure from among all the peoples on earth; for all the earth belongs to me.

6 And you will be my kingdom of priests, my holy nation.' This is the message you must give to the people of Israel."

⁷ So Moses returned from the mountain and called together the elders of the people and told them everything the LORD had commanded him.
⁸ And all the people responded together, "We will do everything the LORD has commanded." So Moses brought the people's answer back to the LORD.

First, Moses went to appear before God. There, the LORD God Almighty gave him instructions for the people. Moses descended from the mountain and told the people what the Lord their God had said. The people responded that they would obey everything their God had commanded.

Moses returned to God with the people's response, and the Lord was noticeably pleased. God was excited that the people were willing to be obedient. Obedience is the secret to power. The Lord validates those who do everything according to His word and follow His instructions.

But there is a revelation in verse 6:

"⁶And you will be my kingdom of priests, my holy nation.' This is the message you must give to the people of Israel."

God was saying to Moses: "It is great that you can come up and commune with me and then go down and speak to the people." But here is what I really want: "I want every one of them to be able to do that. I want a holy nation out of them, where every citizen is a priest."

But this did not materialize in the Old Testament. It became possible in the New Testament after we were washed in the blood of our Lord Jesus Christ.

A Holy Nation

Nobody should be terrified or throw up their arms in despair at this awesome prospect of being a part of a holy nation because the LORD God Almighty had made that provision in Christ Jesus our Saviour. Here is the truth revealed in **Colossians 1:21-22 (KJV):**

²¹And you, that were sometime alienated and enemies in your mind by wicked works, yet now hath he reconciled ²²In the body of his flesh through death, to present you holy and unblameable and unreproveable in his sight:

This is a truth that we must hold dear to our hearts. When we appear before God washed in the blood of our Lord Jesus by faith, we are holy, unblameable, and unreprovable before God. This righteousness comes through faith, given to all who come to God through Christ.

Philippians 3:7-9 (NKJV)

⁷But what things were gain to me, these I have counted loss for Christ. ⁸Yet indeed I also count all things loss for the excellence of the knowledge of Christ Jesus my Lord, for whom I have suffered the loss of all things, and count them as rubbish, that I may gain Christ ⁹and be found in Him, not having my own righteousness, which is from the law, but that which is through faith in Christ, the righteousness which is from God by faith;

This is a powerfully liberating truth. I appear before God not on the basis of my works of righteousness, but washed in the blood of Jesus and clothed in the righteousness of Christ: When I am so covered, I am holy, unblameable, and unreprovable before God. I am sure someone is already wondering: "Is there no more need for personal holiness and righteousness in our daily lives?" Of course, there is. But when we come by faith through Christ, we admit that we can never be good enough to appear before God on our own.

The Prophet Isaiah knew that when he wrote in **Isaiah 64:6 (NLT2)**:

⁶We are all infected and impure with sin. When we display our righteous deeds, they are nothing but filthy rags. Like autumn leaves, we wither and fall, and our sins sweep us away like the wind.

The righteousness that comes through faith causes all recipients who are priests of God to strive daily after holiness, or we would be living a lie. This is the message of **1 John 1:5-7 (NLT2)**:

⁵This is the message we heard from Jesus and now declare to you: God is light, and there is no darkness in him at all. ⁶So we are lying if we say we have fellowship with God but go on living in spiritual darkness; we are not practicing the truth. ⁷ But if we are living in the light, as God is in the light, then we have fellowship with each other, and the Blood of Jesus, his Son, cleanses us from all sin.

If we say we are priests of God who go in and out of the presence of the Almighty and still live daily in the darkness of sin, corruption, and evil, we are liars, for that is not why our Lord Jesus died. Here is why He died, as revealed in **2 Corinthians 5:14-15 (NLT2)**:

¹⁴ Either way, Christ's love controls us. Since we believe that Christ died for all, we also believe that we have all died to our old life. ¹⁵He died for everyone so that those who receive his new life will no longer live for themselves. Instead, they will live for Christ, who died and was raised for them.

Anyone who believes that Christ died to make us holy before God must live Christ's life daily. That is why He died, so He can multiply His life in you and me who believe in Him. It is good to know that there is a very stern warning to anyone and everyone who claims to be in Christ but continues to indulge in willful sinning.

Hebrews 10:26-27 (NLT2)

[26]Dear friends, if we deliberately continue sinning after we have received knowledge of the truth, there is no longer any sacrifice that will cover these sins. [27] There is only the terrible expectation of God's judgment and the raging fire that will consume his enemies.

Men and women who are priests unto God are warned that they will be in danger of chastisement or discipline from God if they do not repent from their sins.

1 Corinthians 11:31-32 (NRSV):

[31]But if we judged ourselves, we would not be judged. [32]But when we are judged by the Lord, we are disciplined so that we may not be condemned along with the world.

The purpose of discipline or chastisement is to teach us to live holy lives like our Lord Jesus. He lived holy while on earth like our Father in heaven is holy:

Hebrews 12:7-10 (NRSV)

[7]Endure trials for the sake of discipline. God is treating you as children; for what child is there whom a parent does not discipline? [8]If you do not have that discipline in which all children share, then you are illegitimate and not his children. [9]Moreover, we had human parents to discipline us, and we respected them. Should we not be even more willing to be subject to the Father of spirits and live? [10]For they disciplined us for a short time as seemed best to them, but he (God) disciplines us for our good, in order that we may share his holiness.

Not only Priests but also Kings

Our priesthood is after the order of Melchizedek because our high priest, our Lord Jesus Christ, is a priest in the order of Melchizedek. **Hebrews 5:5-6 (NRSV):**

⁵So also Christ did not glorify himself in becoming a high priest, but was appointed by the one who said to him, "You are my Son, today I have begotten you"; ⁶as he says also in another place, "You are a priest forever, according to the order of Melchizedek."

As stated earlier, Melchizedek was both king and priest, and his kingship is well-defined for us as King of Righteousness and King of Peace.

The priesthood of the saints who come to God through Christ is after the order of Melchizedek. Therefore, those who come to God through Christ are kings and priests called to be kings of righteousness and peace in their world.

We need this revelation of our priesthood so that we can come into God's presence with boldness by the Blood of Jesus. We enter His presence to be empowered with the anointing to govern.

- We govern by bringing righteousness and peace to our world through our exercise of spiritual authority and power.

CHAPTER 6

SPIRITUAL GOVERNANCE

Job 22:28-30 (KJV)

28 Thou shalt also decree a thing, and it shall be established unto thee: and the light shall shine upon thy ways.
29 When men are cast down, then thou shalt say, There is lifting up; and he shall save the humble person.
30 He shall deliver the island of the innocent: and it is delivered by the pureness of thine hands.

Kings and priests unto God govern by decrees. Their one goal is to establish the will of God on earth as it is in heaven. The rule is that those who want to establish the will of God on earth must live and walk daily in the will of God for their lives. This comes from 2 Corinthians 10:6: *"You will be ready to punish all disobedience when your own obedience is fulfilled."*

When the world's systems around us suffer from pervasive corruption and evil, kings and priests unto God must rise above what prevails so they can force a change from the spiritual to the natural. The weapons we wield are mighty through God. That is a very loaded statement. It means that we can tap into God's boundless capacity to bring about changes in our world through prayer decrees. This is the message of Job 22:28: "You shall decree a thing, and it will be established.

The Holy Spirit and Prayer Decrees

In this context, I say that the Holy Spirit is our spiritual draughtsman. It is based on **Romans 8:26-27 (NKJV)**

26 Likewise, the Spirit also helps in our weaknesses. For we do not know what we should pray for as we ought, but the Spirit Himself makes intercession for us with groanings which cannot be uttered. 27 Now He who searches the hearts knows what the mind of the Spirit is because He makes intercession for the saints according to the will of God.

The Holy Spirit consistently prays in the will of God. There is a simple but all-important prayer question when it comes to prayer decrees:

- LORD, please tell me exactly what to pray and how to pray it so I can connect to Your will on this matter.

We are told that it is only the Holy Spirit that can search and know the mind of God (1 Corinthians 2:10-12).

- When we ask God to teach us what to pray for and give us the words to pray for it, we position ourselves to become effective kings and priests unto God.

This brings me back to that season when our city was plagued by rampant robbery and violence. The Holy Spirit asked me to curse every income earned through robbery and violence. After two weeks of consistently praying this, the head of State changed governors. The new governor introduced Operation Sweep, which swept the robbers away, and the city had peace.

The lesson I took away from that experience is that when we connect with what He wants to hear in prayer and use the words the Spirit has given us, we elicit a response that would surprise us to no end. Compare that to the natural way of organizing a committee that will send a delegation to the state governor or the head of state to do something about the rampant acts of robbery and violence in our city. That just might prove to be an alternative. But not every king and priest can undertake that. But every king and priest can make a prayer decree that will galvanize heaven to bring about changes on the earth. The power we wield is mighty through God (2 Corinthians 10:4). There is no room to speculate on this.

- Choose a specific burden. Ask the Holy Spirit to give you words that connect your prayer decree to God's solution to the situation, and heaven will surprise you.

When we do this multiple times as individuals or groups, we join the many or the few spiritual governors making changes in the world. That is why our Lord Jesus first washed us in His blood to make us holy so we can appear before God Almighty. Then He made us kings and priests unto God.

Spiritual Governors and Persistent Praying

Our Lord Jesus taught us persistent praying in Luke Chapter 18:

Luke 18:1 (KJV)

¹ And he spake a parable unto them to this end, that men ought always to pray, and not to faint;

The parable of the persistent widow is quite instructive. Through persistence, she compelled the unjust judge to answer her. Here is the conclusion our Lord drew from this: **Luke 18:6-8 (NLT2)**

⁶ Then the Lord said, "Learn a lesson from this unjust judge.
⁷ Even he rendered a just decision in the end. So, don't you think God will surely give justice to his chosen people who cry out to him day and night? Will he keep putting them off? 8 I tell you, he will grant justice to them quickly! But when the Son of Man returns, how many will he find on the earth who have faith?"

The reason why persistence in prayer is urged on us by our Lord is because the answer is guaranteed, as we see in this teaching:

Luke 11:9-10 (NLT2)

⁹ "And so I tell you, keep on asking, and you will receive what you ask for. Keep on seeking, and you will find. Keep on knocking, and the door will be opened to you. 10 For everyone who asks, receives. Everyone who seeks, finds. And to everyone who knocks, the door will be opened.

Persistence has a number of signal messages we should know.

- It is through persistence that we show that we believe in the change we are asking for and are ready to wait for it until it comes.
- Heaven orchestrates change. Let us use the first coming of Christ as an example. A man like Simeon prayed for it until the Holy Spirit told him He would certainly see it before he passed on (Luke 2:25-32).

- One reason we see for that delay is the gathering together of what I call the *dramatis personae,* the men and women through whom it will happen. We have Zacharias and Elizabeth to bring in John the Baptist, the forerunner, and Joseph, the husband of Mary, to cover the virgin birth, and Mary to accept to go through the virgin birth. Mary was immortalized by her obedience when she said to Angel Gabriel, "I am the Lord's handmaiden. Let it happen just the way you said (Luke 1:38).

- Persistence also shows that we believe that the authority we have been given works and works consistently well. The delay we see may have to do with divine laws and logistics. With divine laws we have an example in the 400 years wait for the Hebrews to occupy Canaan because the iniquity of the Amorites was not yet complete. Besides, it would take about the same time for a family to become a nation. By the time the Hebrews were leaving Egypt they had acquired the skills they needed to build their own nation. With logistics, we see that successful change has to be orchestrated through men and women who understand the place and power of obedience.

Continuing with the Hebrew story, the LORD told Moses to lead Israel through the south of Egypt to the land of Canaan in the north of Egypt. The reason given in the Bible is so that the people would not encounter wars so early after departure and so run back to Egypt. (Exodus 13:17). But now, we can also see another reason, which is the destruction of the elite Egyptian army at the Red Sea. It is obvious that for as long as the Egyptian army was intact the exodus could easily be reversed by force. To secure the exodus, there had to be a man like Moses who was obedient to God and had been trained to follow instructions through those ten plagues. The more we study the Bible, the more we understand the place of persistence in bringing about change through the will of God.

Through persistence, we show that we understand the difference between God's will and ways and man's will and ways.

Isaiah 55:8-9 (NKJV)

8 "For My thoughts are not your thoughts, Nor are your ways My ways," says the LORD. 9 "For as the heavens are higher than the earth, So are My ways higher than your ways, And My thoughts than your thoughts.

An example is seen in the commissioning of Moses as the deliverer in

Exodus 3:7-10 (NLT2)

7 Then the LORD told him, "I have certainly seen the oppression of my people in Egypt. I have heard their cries of distress because of their harsh slave drivers. Yes, I am aware of their suffering.
8 So, I have come down to rescue them from the power of the Egyptians and lead them out of Egypt into their own fertile and spacious land. It is a land flowing with milk and honey—the land where the Canaanites, Hittites, Amorites, Perizzites, Hivites, and Jebusites now live.
9 Look! The cry of the people of Israel has reached me, and I have seen how harshly the Egyptians abuse them.
10 Now go, for I am sending you to Pharaoh. You must lead my people Israel out of Egypt."

You can almost imagine one of the slaves saying to Moses, "could you please find out from Him when He saw this our state of suffering because we have been in it for a long time."

Through perseverance we show faith and also show that we are prepared to stay with it until it is done. This is why those who say governance prayers must have the mindset of Simeon (Luke 2:25-32), men and women who stay with it until it is done.

Perseverance also sends a message to heaven that we would rather have things go God's way than have them go our way and in our timing. That was the discovery of King David, which he expressed in

2 Samuel 22:29-31 (NKJV)

[29] *"For You are my lamp, O LORD; The LORD shall enlighten my darkness.*
[30] *For by You I can run against a troop; By my God, I can leap over a wall.*
[31] *As for God, His way is perfect; The word of the LORD is proven; He is a shield to all who trust in Him.*

The ways of God are perfect, and so a shepherd boy became the King without rebellion, intrigue, or murders.

Repetition and Governance Prayers

Governance praying is largely decree-making, which is why it can be repetitive. Often, people come to our governance prayer platform and wonder why we repeat our prayers. A governance prayer is an objective-driven prayer. We receive the prayer we should pray and persist in praying it with great expectations until an answer that will bring glory to the Father materializes.

I recall what happened when Covid arrived and was devastating the world. As a medical condition, it was a huge challenge in advanced countries and would be a nightmare in our world. We sought and obtained what decree to make and how to make it. To our surprise and delight, the impact was muted in our world, contrary to every expectation. Then one day, I had a dream and I was wading in a flood that was ankle deep. As I looked up, I noticed that the flood had cut off sharply as if it had a hedge. I was told that this is Covid and that it will end abruptly. I declared the vision on the platform and shared it with a few others outside the platform. Someone told me that pandemics never end abruptly. They usually end after herd immunity has come on board. I countered by saying that this pandemic will be different. Covid ended abruptly. And all the restrictions have been dismantled in the world. Some people say the vaccines helped. It is conceivable that they did, and so possibly is the widespread use of medicines like *Ivermectin* in many nations.

When we say governance prayers, we are not seeking answers in a particular way or by a particular group. When it comes to answers to prayers, the how of the answer is the exclusive preserve of the Almighty God. He orchestrates answers to His glory and to our joy. And that is more than enough for us.

Spiritual Governance and Righteousness

As kings and priests unto God, we must know that we are to pattern what obtains in heaven. The Bible gives us some ideas.

The first is the holiness of God, which is the essence of His nature and being. The Angels daily worship His holiness and majesty as we are told in **Revelation 4:8-11 (NKJV)**

8 The four living creatures, each having six wings, were full of eyes around and within. And they do not rest day or night, saying: "Holy, holy, holy, Lord God Almighty, Who was and is and is to come!" *9 Whenever the living creatures give glory and honor and thanks to Him who sits on the throne, who lives forever and ever, 10 the twenty-four elders fall down before Him who sits on the throne and worship Him who lives forever and ever, and cast their crowns before the throne, saying: 11 "You are worthy, O Lord, To receive glory and honor and power; For You created all things, And by Your will they exist and were created."*

We are also told repeatedly that the foundation of God's throne is righteousness. Righteousness is what confers the authority to govern.

Psalm 89:14 (NKJV)

14 Righteousness and justice are the foundation of Your throne; Mercy and truth go before Your face.

Psalm 97:1-2 (NKJV)

1 The LORD reigns; Let the earth rejoice; Let the multitude of isles be glad!
2 Clouds and darkness surround Him; Righteousness and justice are the foundation of His throne.

Proverbs 16:10-12 (PassionNTPsa)

10 A king speaks the revelation of truth, so he must be extraordinarily careful in the decrees that he makes.
11 The Lord expects you to be fair in every business deal, for he is the one who sets the standards for righteousness.

[12] Kings and leaders despise wrongdoing, for the true authority to rule and reign is built on a foundation of righteousness.

It is for this reason that kings and priests unto God are careful to pursue holiness and righteousness in their lives so they do not invalidate their authority to govern.

All power belongs to God (Psalm 62:11). The LORD God Almighty gave the created angels power, which we call *dunamis*. The Bible reveals that there are hierarchies of angels with different levels of power and authority. There is a passage in the Book of Daniel that reveals the interaction between an emissary angel from God, the prince of the kingdom of Persia on the side of the devil, and the Archangel Michael. The prince of Persia withstood the emissary angel from God for 21 days. Then Archangel Michael appeared on the scene and sent the prince of Persia packing so the emissary angel could come through to deliver God's message to Daniel (Daniel 10:10-14). The process will be repeated by Archangel Michael so the emissary angel can return to heaven (Daniel 10:19-21).

This is evidence from the Bible that quite a lot of invisible activities go on in response to prayer. Let's take a look at this one:

Daniel 10:11-13 (NKJV)

[11] And he said to me, "O Daniel, man greatly beloved, understand the words that I speak to you, and stand upright, for I have now been sent to you." While he was speaking this word to me, I stood trembling. [12] Then he said to me, "Do not fear, Daniel, for from the first day that you set your heart to understand and to humble yourself before your God, your words were heard, and I have come because of your words. [13] But the prince of the kingdom of Persia withstood me twenty-one days; and behold, Michael, one of the chief princes, came to help me, for I had been left alone there with the kings of Persia.

- It is important to note here that the emissary angel was sent by God in response to Daniel's persistent prayers.

This is vital for kings and priests unto God to know. The angel told Daniel that he left to come from heaven the very day that Daniel began his prayers. The delay in his arrival was caused by obstacles from the kingdom of darkness.

Someone reading this may wonder, but how can an angel of the LORD God Almighty be stopped by an agent of the devil? Quite a few lessons come from this:

- The Father chooses which angel to send by the counsel of His own will (Ephesians 1:11b).
- He sent Angel Gabriel to Daniel in Daniel chapter 9:20-23. He flew swiftly for the prince of Persia could not stop him.
- But in Daniel chapter 10, God sent an angel that the prince of Persia could stop. Everything is done after the counsel of God's will.
- In the New Testament, it was the Angel Gabriel who came to Zacharias, the priest in the temple, to announce the coming of John the Baptist, the forerunner. It was the same Angel Gabriel that came to the Virgin Mary to announce the coming of our Lord Jesus Christ through her.
- The conclusion is that the Father knows which hierarchy of Angel to send when delay is ruled out. Everything is done after the counsel of God's will.
- One other very important lesson is that neither angels nor demons can increase the quantum of power given to them by God at their creation. The reason is that creation has finished and will not reopen until God Almighty begins to make all things new (Revelation 21:5).

- That is why kings and priests must hold on to the truth that man is of a higher hierarchy in creation than demons who are fallen angels. We were created a little lower than *Elohim* with authority that uses the Holy Spirit's power for enforcement.

In spiritual governance, as in all other things, we are called to run the divine agenda in God's ways the same way the angels do in heaven.

The Practical Challenge of Governance

Governance decrees are made in the presence of God. This is the lesson we see in **Zechariah 3:6-7 (TEV)**

⁶ Then the angel told Joshua that ⁷ the LORD Almighty had said: "If you obey my laws and perform the duties I have assigned you, then you will continue to be in charge of my Temple and its courts, and I will hear your prayers, just as I hear the prayers of the angels who are in my presence.

Those who have been on our governance prayers platform would have noticed that the first thing we always do is wash ourselves in the blood of Jesus and clothe ourselves fully in the righteousness of our Lord Jesus Christ by faith. It is through such a simple act of faith that we enter into God's presence.

Hebrews 10:19-22 (NIV)

¹⁹ Therefore, brothers, since we have the confidence to enter the Most Holy Place by the blood of Jesus, 20 by a new and living way opened for us through the curtain, that is, his body, 21 and since we have a great priest over the house of God, 22 let us draw near to God with a sincere heart in full assurance of faith, having our hearts sprinkled to cleanse us from a guilty conscience and having our bodies washed with pure water.

Spiritual ways are often simple and uncomplicated. But we must believe the word, receive it, and act on it in simple faith to reap its huge benefits.

But what does it mean to enter through His body? **Philippians 3:9 (NKJV)** provides some insight: ⁹and be found in Him, not having my own righteousness, which is from the law, but that which is through faith in Christ, the righteousness which is from God by faith;

When we enter through His body, we are covered by His righteousness so that we can appear before God holy and blameless.

The reason we appear in God's presence is to receive the Word we are to pray with and the anointing to quicken the Word so we can connect to the divine agenda.

- We should always remember that governance prayers must connect to God's agenda and not to our own ideas, plans, or purposes.

We learn from nature that God is orderly and precise. As spiritual governors, we must seek to fall into the same order. We never create turbulence or disorder. All control is with God our Father. Our Lord Jesus came down from heaven to do the Father's will and not His own. And that is the way we all, as spiritual governors, kings, and priests unto God, must follow.

In summary, we are kings and priests to God, crowned and ordained through Christ's death on the Cross of Calvary.

When we come into God's presence, we are assured that our High Priest is already there to assist us in navigating our primary needs, which are instruction and empowerment. Through instruction, we are told what to do and how to do the will of God in us and through us. Through empowerment, we receive the anointing we need to accomplish the purposes of God Almighty in our lives and in our world.

Kings and Priests and the Anointing

We should always remember that the release of the anointing is God's answer to every need, as revealed to us in **Luke 11:13 (NKJV):**

[13]If you then, being evil, know how to give good gifts to your children, how much more will your heavenly Father give the Holy Spirit to those who ask Him!"

The prophet Isaiah told us that the yoke is always broken because of the anointing (Isaiah 10:27). The Angel Gabriel said to the Virgin Mary that the Holy Spirit would accomplish the divine purpose in her and through her.

Luke 1:34-35 (NKJV).

[34] Then Mary said to the angel, "How can this be since I do not know a man?" [35]And the angel answered and said to her, "The Holy Spirit will come upon you, and the power of the Highest will overshadow you; therefore, also, that Holy One who is to be born will be called the Son of God.

Spiritual governors must actively seek divine empowerment so that God's purposes may be fulfilled. The angel Gabriel said to Mary, "Do not worry. The Holy Spirit will do it."

Our Lord Jesus said to His disciples, "Wait in the city of Jerusalem until the Holy Spirit comes upon you (Luke 24:49)."

We are effective as kings and priests unto God when we learn to walk daily by the Spirit.

When the disciples were threatened by the Jews and warned never again to speak about our Lord Jesus Christ, they knew that the solution was to seek fresh empowerment from heaven.

Acts 4:29-31 (NKJV)

29Now, Lord, look on their threats, and grant to Your servants that with all boldness they may speak Your word, 30by stretching out Your hand to heal, and that signs and wonders may be done through the name of Your holy Servant Jesus." 31And when they had prayed, the place where they were assembled together was shaken; and they were all filled with the Holy Spirit, and they spoke the word of God with boldness.

We see that even at the very beginning of creation, the Holy Spirit was present to accomplish the complexities of the divine purposes, some of which are being unveiled today through molecular Biology, histology, and histochemistry as well as the study of genetics.

Genesis 1:1-2 (NKJV)

1In the beginning, God created the heavens and the earth. 2The earth was without form and void, and darkness was on the face of the deep. And the Spirit of God was hovering over the face of the waters.

Our Lord Jesus said to His disciples, "My words are laden with anointing and power."

John 6:63 (NKJV)

63It is the Spirit who gives life; the flesh profits nothing. The words that I speak to you are spirit, and they are life.

Our Lord Jesus also said in **Luke 8:45-46 (NLT2):**

⁴⁵"Who touched me?" Jesus asked. Everyone denied it, and Peter said, "Master, this whole crowd is pressing up against you." ⁴⁶But Jesus said, "Someone deliberately touched me, for I felt healing power go out from me."

As kings and priests, we must thirst for the Holy Spirit as our Lord Jesus taught us in **John 7:37-39 (NIV)**

³⁷ On the last and greatest day of the Feast, Jesus stood and said in a loud voice, "If anyone is thirsty, let him come to me and drink. 38 Whoever believes in me, as the Scripture has said, streams of living water will flow from within him." ³⁹ By this, he meant the Spirit, whom those who believed in him were later to receive. Up to that time, the Spirit had not been given since Jesus had not yet been glorified.

Elisha certainly did thirst for the Spirit, listening to his request in **2 Kings 2:9 (NKJV).**

⁹And so it was, when they had crossed over, that Elijah said to Elisha, "Ask! What may I do for you before I am taken away from you?" Elisha said, "Please let a double portion of your spirit be upon me."

The prophet Elisha poured water on Elijah's hands, and in the process, he learned the golden rule of ministry—the anointing. As kings and priests unto God, a double portion of anointing must be our thirst and priority.

By way of recap, let us note that when we go before God in prayer with our requests and our needs, the answer is to receive wisdom and instruction and the release of the Spirit that will answer to the need. The Spirit of God can answer to every need because He is the Spirit of creation.

CHAPTER 7

SOVEREIGN GRACE – INDISPENSABLE TO SPIRITUAL GOVERNANCE

This is why we must pause to look at it in detail. The first verses of Zechariah chapter 3 spelled it out very clearly.

Zechariah 3:1-8 (TEV):

¹In another vision, the LORD showed me the High Priest Joshua standing before the angel of the LORD. And there beside Joshua stood Satan, ready to bring an accusation against him. ²The angel of the LORD said to Satan, "May the LORD condemn you, Satan! May the LORD, who loves Jerusalem, condemn you. This man is like a stick snatched from the fire." ³Joshua was standing there, wearing filthy clothes. ⁴The angel said to his heavenly attendants, "Take away the filthy clothes this man is wearing." Then he said to Joshua, "I have taken away your sin and will give you new clothes to wear." ⁵He commanded the attendants to put a clean turban on Joshua's head. They did so, and then they put the new clothes on him while the angel of the LORD stood there.

⁶Then the angel told Joshua that ⁷the LORD Almighty had said: "If you obey my laws and perform the duties I have assigned you, then you will continue to be in charge of my Temple and its courts, and I will hear your prayers, just as I hear the prayers of the angels who are in my presence. ⁸Listen then, Joshua, you who are the High Priest; and listen, you fellow priests of his, you that are the sign of a good future: I will reveal my servant, who is called The Branch!

We may have made reference to this passage earlier, but now we pause to savor the significance of what is revealed here. What this passage reveals is that before we are empowered, we must be cleansed from all sin. There was a hint in Exodus 3:5, when God said to Moses, "You are standing on holy ground). The prophet Isaiah was the first to reveal that cleansing from sin must precede empowerment and commissioning. Take a look at **Isaiah 6:5-9 (NKJV).**

⁵So I said: "Woe is me, for I am undone! Because I am a man of unclean lips, And I dwell in the midst of a people of unclean lips; For my eyes have seen the King, The LORD of hosts." ⁶Then one of the seraphim flew to me, having in his hand a live coal which he had taken with the tongs from the altar. ⁷And he touched my mouth with it, and said: "Behold, this has touched your lips; Your iniquity is taken away, And your sin purged." ⁸Also I heard the voice of the Lord, saying: "Whom shall I send, And who will go for Us?" Then I said, "Here am I! Send me." ⁹And He said, "Go, and tell this people: 'Keep on hearing, but do not understand; Keep on seeing, but do not perceive.'

In the above vision, the prophet Isaiah realized that oftentimes, our worship is in ignorance. We live filthy lives and try to worship a holy God. This is why there must always be cleansing before the call and before commissioning. In Zechariah chapter 3, Joshua, the high priest, came before the LORD for empowerment. The devil came alongside him to accuse him before God. This is the power and significance of the Blood of the Lamb revealed in **Revelation 12:10-11 (NKJV).**

[10]Then I heard a loud voice saying in heaven, "Now salvation, and strength, and the kingdom of our God, and the power of His Christ have come, for the accuser of our brethren, who accused them before our God day and night, has been cast down. [11]And they overcame him by the blood of the Lamb and by the word of their testimony, and they did not love their lives to the death.

The accuser is busy before God, ensuring that we are not empowered. He is permitted to accuse and obstruct us because of the sins we commit in our lives. But what our Father in heaven did was to provide sovereign grace through the Blood of Jesus, which cleanses us from all sins. But what happened to Joshua was long before Christ. That tells us that sovereign grace has always been in operation.

In the case of Joshua, let us look closely at what happened in **Zechariah 3:3-5 (TEV):**

[3]Joshua was standing there, wearing filthy clothes. [4]The angel said to his heavenly attendants, "Take away the filthy clothes this man is wearing." Then he said to Joshua, "I have taken away your sin and will give you new clothes to wear." [5]He commanded the attendants to put a clean turban on Joshua's head. They did so, and then they put the new clothes on him while the angel of the LORD stood there.

Sovereign grace is about mercy undeserved. Joshua was cleansed by mercy and grace and so was positioned for empowerment.

Obedience, the Bedrock of Empowerment
Zechariah 3:6-8 (TEV)

⁶Then the angel told Joshua that ⁷the LORD Almighty had said: "If you obey my laws and perform the duties I have assigned you, then you will continue to be in charge of my Temple and its courts, and I will hear your prayers, just as I hear the prayers of the angels who are in my presence. ⁸Listen then, Joshua, you who are the High Priest; and listen, you fellow priests of his, you that are the sign of a good future: I will reveal my servant, who is called The Branch!

There is a great revelation here for all of us who desire to be empowered on earth to fulfill God's plans and purposes in our lives as kings and priests unto God.

- "Hear this, Joshua, for you to be empowered, you must obey My laws. You must perform the duties I have assigned you."

What does that mean to us today? What duties has He assigned to us? It is to build the Kingdom of God and righteousness in the lives of men and women. This is the message of **Luke 17:20-21 (TEV)**:

²⁰Some Pharisees asked Jesus when the Kingdom of God would come. His answer was, "The Kingdom of God does not come in such a way as to be seen. ²¹No one will say, 'Look, here it is!' or, 'There it is!'; because the Kingdom of God is within you."

Quite a few Scriptures tell us what our duty is as kings and priests unto God on earth. Here is what our Lord Jesus said to His disciples:

Matthew 6:31-33 (NIV)

³¹ So do not worry, saying, 'What shall we eat?' or 'What shall we drink?' or 'What shall we wear?' 32 For the pagans run after all these things, and your heavenly Father knows that you need them. 33 But seek first his kingdom and his righteousness, and all these things will be given to you as well.

The way to go about it is to conform to the image of Christ so we can do it the way He did it.

Romans 8:29-30 (NKJV):

[29]For whom He foreknew, He also predestined to be conformed to the image of His Son, that He might be the firstborn among many brethren. [30]Moreover whom He predestined, these He also called; whom He called, these He also justified; and whom He justified, these He also glorified.

We are to bring sons and daughters of God to glory through conformity with the image and character of Christ.

Let us note that there is a clear distinction between building the kingdom of man and building the Kingdom of God.

- When we build the kingdom of man, the focus is on the organization, its size, its structures and tentacles as well as its material resources.
- When we build the Kingdom of God, our focus changes to raising men and women who follow Christ and daily conform to His image.

In the Kingdom of God, it is not about size and numbers but about transformation, discipleship, and conformity to the image and character of Christ. Our Lord Jesus ministered to thousands but left just 11 disciples to propagate the Gospel of the Kingdom of God.

The Secret to Continued Empowerment

The secret is in **Zechariah 3:7b**.

And I will hear your prayers, just as I hear the prayers of the angels who are in My presence.

Unquestioning loyalty and obedience to God are the secret keys to continued empowerment. We have access to His presence when we are purged of our sins. When we obey Him, He answers our prayers and so empowers us to fulfill our calling on the earth. Brethren, there is no mystery here but a simple truth revealed by our Lord Jesus Christ. Let us look at a few scriptures:

- The Son can do nothing of Himself.

John 5:19-20 (NKJV)

[19]Then Jesus answered and said to them, "Most assuredly, I say to you, the Son can do nothing of Himself, but what He sees the Father do; for whatever He does, the Son also does in like manner. [20]For the Father loves the Son, and shows Him all things that He Himself does; and He will show Him greater works than these, that you may marvel.

- The Son always pleases the Father.

John 8:28-29 (NKJV)

[28]Then Jesus said to them, "When you lift up the Son of Man, then you will know that I am He, and that I do nothing of Myself; but as My Father taught Me, I speak these things. [29]And He who sent Me is with Me. The Father has not left Me alone, for I always do those things that please Him."

- This is the way I show the world that I love the Father by My obedience.

John 14:29-31 (NKJV)

[29]And now I have told you before it comes, that when it does come to pass, you may believe. [30]I will no longer talk much with you, for the ruler of this world is coming, and he has nothing in Me. [31]But that the world may know that I love the Father, and as the Father gave Me commandment, so I do. Arise, let us go from here.

There is no magic to empowerment by God. The secret is an open one. Through cleansing and obedience, we position ourselves for commissioning and empowerment. Any believer in God through Christ can do this and function effectively as a king and priest unto God on the earth.

The Signs of a Good Future

The doctrine of seed time and harvest time was embedded in nature by the Lord God Almighty as an eternal principle in **Genesis 8:22 (NKJV):**

[22]"While the earth remains, seedtime and harvest, cold and heat, winter and summer, and day and night shall not cease."

This was taken beyond agriculture through **Galatians 6:7-8 (NKJV)**

[7]Do not be deceived, God is not mocked; for whatever a man sows, that he will also reap. [8]For he who sows to his flesh will of the flesh reap corruption, but he who sows to the Spirit will of the Spirit reap everlasting life.

The high priest Joshua and his fellow priests are the signs of a good future.

Zechariah 3:8:

8Listen then, Joshua, you who are the High Priest; and listen, you fellow priests of his, you that are the sign of a good future: I will reveal my servant, who is called The Branch!

The signs of a good future are not the mineral deposits in the nation as important as that is. Great economic plans are not the signs of a good future, as important as these are. Highly educated men and women are not the signs of a good future as indispensable as they are.

- The signs of a good future in any nation are the men and women who fear God, stay away from evil, and work righteousness on the earth. They serve God and man as kings and priests unto God. They are kings of righteousness and peace on the earth, no matter their vocation, business, or calling.

So, it is not about great plans and highly qualified people. It is about godly men and women with high moral and ethical integrity who fear God and work for righteousness, equity, and justice on the earth.

They are to be found among the empowered priests in Zechariah chapter 3.

The Branch has come, and He has made us kings and priests unto His God so that you and I can become the signs of a good future for our nations in every generation.

CHAPTER 8

THE POWER OF
THE REMNANT
CHURCH

Isaiah 1:9 (NKJV)

⁹ Unless the LORD of hosts Had left to us a very small remnant, We would have become like Sodom, We would have been made like Gomorrah.

The prophet Isaiah wrote about the remnants that were left to sustain the vision of a messianic kingdom coming through the lineage of King David. Through the intercession of the patriarch Abraham, we see the place and power of the remnant Church. Let us go there immediately.

Genesis 18:23-26 (NKJV)

²³ And Abraham came near and said, "Would You also destroy the righteous with the wicked? ²⁴ Suppose there were fifty righteous within the city; would You also destroy the place and not spare it for the fifty righteous that were in it? ²⁵ *Far be it from You to do such a thing as this, to slay the righteous with the wicked, so that the righteous should be as the wicked; far be it from You! Shall not the Judge of all the earth do right?"* ²⁶ *So the LORD said, "If I find in Sodom fifty righteous within the city, then I will spare all the place for their sakes."*

The power of the remnant Church is in that 26ᵗʰ verse and similar verses: *If I find in Sodom fifty righteous within the city, then I will spare all the place for their sakes."*

This tells us the power of righteous living before God. From Abraham's intercession, we gain the idea of a minimum.

Genesis 18:32 (NKJV)

³² *Then he said, "Let not the Lord be angry, and I will speak but once more: Suppose ten should be found there?" And He said, "I will not destroy it for the sake of ten."*

Abraham started with fifty righteous persons. When he learned that Sodom did not have fifty righteous persons, he reduced his number to forty-five, arguing that the loss of five persons should not make a difference. However, when he was told that Sodom did not have ten righteous persons within it, Abraham gave up.

Understanding Righteousness Before God

There is a difference between a righteous person before God and sinless perfection. The definition of sinless perfection was given to us in the Book of Hebrews:

Hebrews 4:15 (NKJV)

15 For we do not have a High Priest who cannot sympathize with our weaknesses, but was in all points tempted as we are, yet without sin.

Tempted in every way but without sin was the life lived by our Lord Jesus Christ while He was here on earth. We learn from here that temptation is not a sin until we yield to it.

The Book of James tells us that there is a kind of progression from temptation to sin.

James 1:13-16 (KJV)

13 Let no man say when he is tempted, I am tempted of God: for God cannot be tempted with evil, neither tempteth he any man: 14 But every man is tempted, when he is drawn away of his own lust, and enticed. 15 Then when lust hath conceived, it bringeth forth sin: and sin, when it is finished, bringeth forth death. 16 Do not err, my beloved brethren.

Indeed, a person may sorely be tempted but still find grace to say No. But because of the weakness in our nature, we find that occasionally we may find ourselves succumbing to temptation. We may then find ourselves sinning in thought, word, or deed. How, then, do we describe righteousness before God? The answer we also find in the Book of Hebrews.

Hebrews 5:12-14 (NIV)

12 In fact, though by this time you ought to be teachers, you need someone to teach you the elementary truths of God's word all over again. You need milk, not solid food! 13 Anyone who lives on milk, being still an infant, is not acquainted with the teaching about righteousness. 14 But solid food is for the mature, who by constant use have trained themselves to distinguish good from evil.

Righteous living before God belongs to the spiritually mature who have their senses well instructed to distinguish right from wrong. They are not in the habit of doing what they know is wrong. They do not follow the natural man to rationalize their way out of a guilty conscience in order to justify their actions in their own eyes.

The Righteous and Genuine Repentance

King David was a man after God's heart. He showed us what to do when we fail after his adultery with Bathsheba and the subsequent murder of her husband came to light.

2 Samuel 12:11-13 (NKJV)

[11] Thus says the LORD: 'Behold, I will raise up adversity against you from your own house; and I will take your wives before your eyes and give them to your neighbor, and he shall lie with your wives in the sight of this sun. [12] For you did it secretly, but I will do this thing before all Israel, before the sun.' " [13] So David said to Nathan, "I have sinned against the LORD." And Nathan said to David, "The LORD also has put away your sin; you shall not die.

Subsequently, King David wrote his great confessional to reveal the depth of his penitence and his plea for forgiveness in Psalm 51. Some of the verses are quite revealing:

Psalm 51:1-4 (NKJV)

[1] Have mercy upon me, O God, According to Your lovingkindness; According to the multitude of Your tender mercies, Blot out my transgressions.
[2] Wash me thoroughly from my iniquity, And cleanse me from my sin.
[3] For I acknowledge my transgressions And my sin is always before me.

⁴ Against You, You only, have I sinned, And done this evil in Your sight-- That You may be found just when You speak, And blameless when You judge.

Godly sorrow is at the heart of genuine repentance. King David showed deep godly sorrow here. Writing to the Corinthian Church, the Apostle Paul noted that godly sorrow will always lead to genuine repentance and salvation of the soul of man (2 Corinthians 7:10).

Psalm 51:9-12 (NKJV)

⁹ Hide Your face from my sins, And blot out all my iniquities.
¹⁰ Create in me a clean heart, O God, And renew a steadfast spirit within me.
¹¹ Do not cast me away from Your presence, And do not take Your Holy Spirit from me.
¹² Restore to me the joy of Your salvation, And uphold me by Your generous Spirit.

King David greatly feared the consequences of his sin, particularly what it would do to his personal relationship with God.

Psalm 51:14 (NKJV)

¹⁴ Deliver me from the guilt of bloodshed, O God, The God of my salvation, And my tongue shall sing aloud of Your righteousness.

Forgiveness of our sins is all about God's mercy. King David acknowledged his sins before God. This is the habit of a righteous person. Many may condemn and deride him, including those who do the same things in their lives. But that should not make us hide our sins before God. We are told that he who covers his sins will not prosper, but whoever confesses and forsakes them will have mercy (Proverbs 28:13).

Psalm 51:16-17 (NKJV)

16 For You do not desire sacrifice, or else I would give it; You do not delight in burnt offering.
17 The sacrifices of God are a broken spirit, A broken and a contrite heart-- These, O God, You will not despise.

A large offering in cash or kind is not a substitute for genuine repentance. I always remind myself and others that God does not spend money or ride in expensive cars. King David reminded us that what He is looking for is a broken spirit and a contrite heart. Genuine contrition helps ensure that we do not repeat the same thing.

Repentance for a righteous person is *godly sorrow* that powers a complete rethink of our life and our ways, leading to salvation or change. It is to King David's credit that his genuine repentance made him stay away from immorality and its complications.

That is why genuine repentance must always be accompanied by a change of ways. Without the change of ways, repentance is not genuine.

False Repentance

King David was not the only one ever to have declared, "I have sinned against the LORD." The Pharaoh of Egypt said the same to Moses:

Exodus 10:16-17 (NKJV)

16 Then Pharaoh called for Moses and Aaron in haste and said, "I have sinned against the LORD your God and against you. 17 Now therefore, please forgive my sin only this once, and entreat the LORD your God, that He may take away from me this death only."

Pharaoh's acknowledgment of his sin was a ploy to stop the plague. He had no intention of changing his heart of rebellion against God.

Balaam, the prophet, also declared that he had sinned but was not seriously contemplating returning or changing his ways.

Numbers 22:34-35 (NLT2)

34 Then Balaam confessed to the angel of the LORD, "I have sinned. I didn't realize you were standing in the road to block my way. I will return home if you are against my going."
35 But the angel of the LORD told Balaam, "Go with these men, but say only what I tell you to say." So Balaam went on with Balak's officials.

What Balaam said to the angel revealed his heart's eagerness to go and collect Balak's honorarium. "If you are displeased… what an if." The angel was there to convey God's displeasure in vivid language. Yet Balaam could still say, "If you are displeased." How else can you assess divine displeasure when your donkey was speaking to you with the voice of a man?

What these examples of false repentance reveal is that it is not about what we say but about contrition and change that is in our hearts.

The righteous man can distinguish between right and wrong and is always in the habit of choosing right over wrong. If he commits the error of choosing wrong over right, he turns around in genuine repentance accompanied by the determination never to go that route again.

The God we serve sees the heart and knows its thoughts and intentions. Anyone who is a friend of God should be in a position to sense divine displeasure. This is why it is nearly impossible to speak about righteousness for another.

The Spirit of Eternal Vigilance

Kings and priests unto God must know that, like Joshua and his priests, we are the signs of a good future for our nations. As a result, it is our duty to maintain constant vigilance over our lives. We must guard our hearts with all diligence, for out of it are the issues of life (Proverbs 4:23). This is the word our Lord Jesus gave to His disciples in the Garden of Gethsemane:

Matthew 26:41 (KJV)

41 Watch and pray that ye enter not into temptation: the spirit indeed is willing, but the flesh is weak.

Our constant companion in this vigilance is the Holy Spirit. He will mortify our flesh and lead us in all areas so that we make the right decisions and avoid unnecessary temptations and pitfalls. Our Lord Jesus was led by the Holy Spirit in all things, and so must we.

Growing the Remnant Church

Only the remnant Church can make the difference before God. They are positioned to become effective kings and priests unto God. Therefore, it is vital to continually grow the remnants in the body of Christ, men and women who strive to walk daily in the footprints of our Lord Jesus. One sure way to grow the remnant Church is to follow the spirit and letter of the Great Commission as recorded by Matthew the Gospel writer:

Matthew 28:18-20 (KJV)

18 And Jesus came and spake unto them, saying, All power is given unto me in heaven and in earth. 19 Go ye therefore, and teach all nations, baptizing them in the name of the Father, and of the Son, and of the Holy Ghost: 20 Teaching them to observe all things whatsoever I have commanded you: and, lo, I am with you alway, even unto the end of the world. Amen.

The commission is to go and **teach** all nations.

After you have taught them, baptize them.

After you have baptized them, further **teach them to observe all things whatsoever I have commanded you**.

This is the way to grow kings and priests unto God, men and women who have personal loyalties to God and are determined to yield themselves to grow and prosper the Kingdom of God in the lives of their fellow men and women.

CHAPTER 9

SEPARATION, CONSECRATION, AND SANCTIFICATION FOR

KINGS AND PRIESTS UNTO GOD

John 17:15-19 (NKJV)

¹⁵ I do not pray that You should take them out of the world, but that You should keep them from the evil one. ¹⁶ They are not of the world, just as I am not of the world. ¹⁷ Sanctify them by Your truth. Your word is truth. ¹⁸ As You sent Me into the world, I also have sent them into the world. ¹⁹ And for their sakes I sanctify Myself, that they also may be sanctified by the truth.

One of the great mysteries of the Kingdom of God on the earth is that our Lord Jesus put on flesh and became human in the womb of Mary. To what purpose? It is so that He would become exactly like us. He left the privileges and powers of divinity behind so that He would function on earth as a man filled with the Holy Spirit and not as God. He wants us to know that we should function just like He did, simply kings and priests, men and women filled, controlled, and led in all things by the Spirit of God.

Just before He went to the Cross, the Apostle John recorded that He prayed for His disciples and us.

SEPARATION FROM THE WORLD

Here is the prayer for separation from the world in John Chapter 17, verses 15 and 16 above:

15 I do not pray that You should take them out of the world, but that You should keep them from the evil one. 16 They are not of the world, just as I am not of the world.

As kings and priests unto God, we are called to be in the world but not of the world. This is the order to stay out of the philosophy of men and women in the world who mind earthly things and seek fame and fortune as an end. When kings and priests are blessed with fame and fortune in their endeavors, it is so that they will deploy their position, wealth, and influence to further the Kingdom of God in the lives of men and women on the earth.

In some circles, it is called *moderation* in all things. Any success a king and priest achieves in life is offered on the altar to the Father and King to use to further the Kingdom of God on the earth.

Separation and moderation are tough, but both are distinguishing hallmarks of kings and priests to God on earth. Only the Holy Spirit can lead us daily to achieve both.Our Lord Jesus practiced Separation

It is natural to wonder how He could have so much spiritual power and authority yet wielded them with so much control. The answer He revealed when He said, "The Son can do nothing of Himself except what He sees the Father do (John 5:19)."

The way to read this is that He did not set out to achieve separation from the world as a goal. But as He followed in the footsteps of our Father in heaven, His life revealed separation from the world. He was in the world but not of the world.

This is the only way that kings and priests unto God can achieve the same result. When the Spirit of God leads us in all things, we discover with time that our lives reveal and daily reveal separation from the world.

To show how difficult this can be for the individual who is not led by the Spirit of God, we have Scriptures that testify to the struggle:

1 Corinthians 5:9-11 (NLT2)

⁹ When I wrote to you before, I told you not to associate with people who indulge in sexual sin. ¹⁰ But I wasn't talking about unbelievers who indulge in sexual sin, or are greedy, or cheat people, or worship idols. You would have to leave this world to avoid people like that. ¹¹ I meant that you are not to associate with anyone who claims to be a believer yet indulges in sexual sin, or is greedy, or worships idols, or is abusive, or is a drunkard, or cheats people. Don't even eat with such people.

Take a look at this: As kings and priests unto God, we interact with unbelievers to bring the Light of the life of Jesus into their lives so that the Kingdom of God and its righteousness will become the active and dominating principle of their lives. But if a brother or sister manifests the character and attributes regularly seen in unbelievers, we must separate from the fellow. The reason is obvious.

For example, if a brother or sister brings the ways of the world amongst separated kings and priests unto God, the community of separated souls will risk getting entangled again with the world and its ways if they don't separate from him.

The Apostle Paul likened the brother bearing this corrupting influence to yeast. If you do not separate from him or her sooner rather than later, his/her ways will negatively impact the entire group.

Here is a simple example. A community of saints believe and practice chastity. For them, there is no place for sex before marriage. Then, a supposed brother and sister join them, and he and his girlfriend spend nights and weekends in each other's apartment regularly. When such behavior was noticed and challenged, their response was that they planned to get married shortly and so did not see any need to wait. They insisted that they were not doing anything wrong, and before you could say, "Wait a moment," the practice had become the lifestyle of many in the group.

Separation from the world and its ways is separation from what the Bible calls the pleasures of sin (Hebrews 11:25). Because they are pleasures that satisfy the flesh, kings and priests unto God must separate or else find themselves back in the grips and slavery of diverse lusts. The same goes for many worldly practices like bribery and corruption and the like sharp and shady business practices.

Separation and Sanctification by the Truth

This is imperative for kings and priests unto God if they are to wield spiritual power and authority in the world. If we do not separate from the world and its ways, then we cannot be light-bearers driving away darkness from the world.

This is why it is a tough call to be a king and a priest to God on earth. Nobody can live the life of a saint without the power and control of the Holy Spirit. And what the Holy Spirit does is lead us away from things we cannot handle because we lack the inner strength and maturity required. He also leads us away from the peril of carnal ambitions inspired by the world and its ways. He keeps us on the path of God's will for our lives and guides us to achieve success that will not derail our separation from the world.

A young man came to me some years ago to testify that life was very tough for him after his National Youth Service. He could not find a job and suffered quite a bit with much frustration. Then, suddenly, everything changed after a multinational group employed him. Before I could finish rejoicing with him, he told me there was a different kind of problem now. The young ladies were paying him a lot of attention, and that was proving a big challenge.

For this and many other reasons, we must be sanctified by the truth as it is in the Bible. No matter how successful our lives become, our principles of separation from the world and its ways must not change.

Every time we struggle to keep the ways of the world out of our lives, it is proof that the enemy is plotting to eliminate us as effective soldiers of Christ. If we yield to the pressure, the result would be to shut our mouths and quench our lights, eliminating us as light-bearers in the world and as effective kings and priests unto God.

One only needs to look around to notice many that have lost their voices against evil ways and whose light has become very dim or totally dead.

Oftentimes, when you hear men describe someone as a motivational speaker, what they are referring to is their capacity to awaken the lazy and unambitious to struggle for the good things in life, which is not bad in itself. But what the body of Christ badly needs is to motivate kings and priests to walk the straight and narrow road while striving to maximize their potential in life. This can only be achieved as we are led by the Holy Spirit in all things.

CHAPTER 10

KINGS AND PRIESTS AND IMPORTUNITY

Our relationship with God should be such that it gives us boldness before Him. This lesson on importunity was taught alongside the lesson on prayer by our Lord Jesus Christ. We are to pray to our Father in heaven. Our primary desire is to see His will done on earth as it is done in heaven. As kings and priests seeking to see God's will be done on earth while shielding ourselves from pernicious evil, we are called to show persistence and consistent intensity, knowing that the God who has called us to pray and work is both willing and able to answer our prayers and empower us to work effectively.

Luke 11:5-8 (KJV)

5 And he said unto them, Which of you shall have a friend, and shall go unto him at midnight, and say unto him, Friend, lend me three loaves; 6 For a friend of mine in his journey is come to me, and I have nothing to set before him? 7 And he from within shall answer and say, Trouble me not: the door is now shut, and my children are with me in bed; I cannot rise and give thee. [8] I say unto you, Though he will not rise and give him, because he is his friend, yet because of his importunity he will rise and give him as many as he needeth.

What is Importunity?

Let us take in the scenario of this parable. There is a need. There is desperation. The petitioner is not asking for self but for the benefit of another whose situation was desperate. And so, he comes with shameless persistence at an odd hour and would not take no for an answer.

Our Lord Jesus superimposes that scenario in our world. We, as kings and priests unto God are desperately seeking to bring salvation to the souls of men and women on earth held captive by the devil. The situation is desperate as men and women disappear to hell every minute.

Our heavenly Father is willing, available, and able to give the Holy Spirit to those who ask Him so that we would arise to dismantle the kingdom of darkness and plant the Kingdom of God's marvelous Light in its place.

When Abraham interceded for Sodom and reached 'ten people' in Genesis 18, he must have felt that the situation in Sodom was totally hopeless.

In the end, how many righteous people were in Sodom and Gomorrah? Only Lot, his wife, and two daughters. That's four persons, and even the four were very questionable because Lot's wife had her heart in the sinful city. When they were leaving Sodom, she must have felt like, "Eh! You know this righteousness palaver, there'll be no more parties and groovy times." Then, she looked back in disobedience to the angel's instruction and turned into a pillar of salt. So, Lot's wife didn't make it.

Now, even the children's righteousness was questionable. They had left all the men in Sodom, and they reasoned that their father had to be their husband. So, in fact, only one person was righteous, Lot, and Abraham was looking for ten 2 Peter 2:7-8). Only one person's heart was right with God because for Lot's daughters to get their father to sleep with them, they had to make him drunk.

Therefore, it is clear that it is not easy to find righteous men and women who are friends of God.

- The determination of everyone who comes to Church should be, "I must be one of the righteous men and women in this place. Yes, it doesn't matter what is happening; it doesn't matter what everybody else is doing. I must be one of those people that God can find and say, "Because you are here, let the Angel of death and destruction pass by." That's the power of the righteous man before God.

Quite a few people are mystified by Nigeria's survival despite all the horrors that go on here. Let us note that it is not about the number of righteous men and women within it; what should concern us is the determination and desire to be numbered among them. It is within our power to be numbered among them.

The message of kings and priests unto God is to awaken the dead bones in the Body of Christ to rise to become a mighty army fighting for the Kingdom of God and its righteousness in our world.

The lesson on importunity is to let us know that kings and priests have power with God, which we can release through persistent prayer. Nobody may know your name. You may not be numbered among the religious elite of the society. But each time you bow your heart to the LORD in prayer, heaven sends answers that establish the will and purposes of God. And that's what matters.

Sometimes, what we see is the reality of the process. The Apostle Paul said to his fellow travelers in Acts 27, "The ship and the cargo will be lost, but nobody will die. Before we get to Rome, our destination, we shall be cast on a certain island." That is what I call the process.

Paul was the king and priest who stood in the gap before God for the travelers on that ship. Those who learn to wait before God reduce the weeping before the world. Through the exercise of spiritual authority and power, kings and priests learn to scatter the gathering clouds of evil forces so the plans and purposes of our God can run unhindered by men and devils.

The lessons from the prophet Isaiah here are always relevant:

Isaiah 55:6-9 (GW)

[6] *Seek the LORD while he may be found. Call on him while he is near.* [7] *Let wicked people abandon their ways. Let evil people abandon their thoughts. Let them return to the LORD, and he will show compassion to them. Let them return to our God, because he will freely forgive them.* [8] *"My thoughts are not your thoughts, and my ways are not your ways," declares the LORD.* [9] *"Just as the heavens are higher than the earth, so my ways are higher than your ways, and my thoughts are higher than your thoughts."*

As kings and priests, we learn to wait and see how God answers our prayers, sometimes through expected ways and sometimes through unexpected ways. We learn that it is not about precedents but about sovereignty.

The call to rise and become a king and a priest unto God is so that you and I can be one of the many or the few who stand in the gap to wield spiritual governance authority that keeps the community or the nation going in spite of everything. I have lived through many near disasters due to the many evil ploys of rulers and leaders. But as we stood in the gap and prayed, the LORD had mercy on our land and shielded us from much harm.

Let us join hands for there is much wickedness and evil in our nation that is calling for advertised and unadvertised intercessors. Nobody needs to know your name or mine. But where we are in our little corners, the Holy Spirit has raised us up as spiritual governors who wield much authority where it matters, which is before our Father in heaven. From His mercy seat, mercy will flow down to stave off disasters.

Abraham got to ten righteous people and stopped. We do not need to speculate on how many righteous people are needed for where we are. All that is needed is for us to be one of them and encourage friends and family to rise up to the challenge and join the ranks of kings and priests in their world. As we encourage others to rise and become kings and priests unto God our Father, the number of righteous men and women available to God will grow where we are.

There is one thing we need to know: things don't just happen; people make them happen. That's what kings and priests are all about. You don't give credit to luck for the peace you experience as a nation. Often, you'd hear people say, "Ah! We are very lucky o!"

Indeed! Luck is an indifferent destiny. Kings and priests unto God pray according to the will of the Father to secure peace and stability in their world. They depend on the Holy Spirit to make the decrees that impact their world effective. One thing we must know is that the challenges are many and the prayer decrees needed even more. That is why many kings and priests are needed so that the Holy Spirit can share the burden. As one group is focusing on one area with dedication and passion, another group is doing the same in another area. We are called to be kings and priests unto God so that we will not be bystanders and observers watching events. Instead, we will be making things happen in our world and bringing down God's will on our world.

Importunity

How could Abraham be so bold before the Lord God of all heaven and earth? The answer is that he knew God enough to know what to say before Him. Let's listen to him:

Genesis 18:24-26 (NRSV)

24 Suppose there are fifty righteous within the city; will you then sweep away the place and not forgive it for the fifty righteous who are in it? 25 Far be it from you to do such a thing, to slay the righteous with the wicked, so that the righteous fare as the wicked! Far be that from you! Shall not the Judge of all the earth do what is just?" 26 And the LORD said, "If I find at Sodom fifty righteous in the city, I will forgive the whole place for their sake."

Abraham knew that righteousness is the foundation of God's throne and so he used that to pray. He was a friend of God. We become friends of God when we trust and obey Him and walk daily in His will. Friendship with God is not a privilege reserved for the few but an open door through which any can enter, provided they are ready to trust and obey the LORD like Abraham.

James 2:23 (NRSV)

3 Thus the scripture was fulfilled that says, "Abraham believed God, and it was reckoned to him as righteousness," and he was called the friend of God.

Importance has its roots in our relationship with God. It is not a gift or a blessing bestowed. It is reserved for those who love God and obey Him, and any of us can draw close to God to become His friend. God is not partial (Acts 10:34).

Friendship with God is not like a family relationship. Family relationships are imposed on us. You grow up, and one comes to say to you, "You see that one? He's your cousin. Do you see that other one? She's your niece." Then, you welcome them.

They introduce relatives to us. But nobody can call you and say, "You see that man, he's your friend." Nobody shows you your friend. So, when they say a man is a friend of God, it's a cultivated relationship. You know how you live daily to do as He says. God knows the heart with which you do as He says. That's what made Abraham very bold. You can go into a place and they request for a set of tumblers to serve water to the guests. Then, the people report, "We went to that house there, and they said to us 'No, we don't give out our tumblers.'"

Then a man asks, "Which house? Mr. Johnson's?"

"Yes," someone responds.

With confidence, he answers, "Don't worry, I will get them." Then he goes over there and comes out with the tumblers. What made the difference? He knows the Johnson family, and they know and trust him. He is their friend.

That is why we say that the Church is an academy where men and women are taught to be friends with God through faith, loyalty, and obedience.

Importunity is also about righteousness before God. The psalmist tells us that God loves the righteous (Psalm 146:8). The Bible also says that God is righteous and loves righteous deeds:

Psalm 11:7 (HCSB)

For the LORD is righteous; He loves righteous deeds. The upright will see His face.

Those who are upright in their ways are welcome in His presence. They are the friends of God.

Therefore, we must determine in our hearts to be friends of God so that the Kingdom of God will prosper in our hands. Friendship has huge benefits. Even in normal human relationships, there are friends that you'll go to, and whatever you need that they have, you're sure to get it because of the bond of friendship between you.

Kings and Priests as Friends of God

When we search the Bible, we see that friendship with God has huge benefits. That is why Abraham's family workers defeated a confederacy of kings in battle. Let's take a look at Genesis 14. To cut a long story short, Abraham was told that four kings gathered against five kings. They destroyed the five kings and carried away the people there. Among those carried away were Lot and his family. Abraham gathered his household staff, and the servants born in his house together and gave chase. He defeated them and brought back the captives, including Lot, his nephew. How can a household army defeat a confederacy of four kings with their armies? Here is the reason, in

Genesis 14:18-20 (NKJV)

18 Then Melchizedek king of Salem brought out bread and wine; he was the priest of God Most High. 19 And he blessed him and said: "Blessed be Abram of God Most High, Possessor of heaven and earth;
20 And blessed be God Most High, Who has delivered your enemies into your hand." And he gave him a tithe of all.

Melchizedek, the priest of the Most High God told Abraham that his family army defeated this confederacy of four kings because the unseen armies of God deployed on his side. Such is the power of friendship with God.

The Army of Heaven Deploys, but on whose Side?

Through Joshua, Moses' successor, we learn a vital lesson on how to get God on our side

Joshua 5:13-15 (NRSV)

13 Once when Joshua was by Jericho, he looked up and saw a man standing before him with a drawn sword in his hand. Joshua went to him and said to him, "Are you one of us, or one of our adversaries?"
14 He replied, "Neither; but as commander of the army of the LORD I have now come." And Joshua fell on his face to the earth and worshiped, and he said to him, "What do you command your servant, my lord?" 15 The commander of

the army of the LORD said to Joshua, "Remove the sandals from your feet, for the place where you stand is holy." And Joshua did so.

It is important to know on whose side heaven deploys because kings and priests unto God will fight diversities of battles in their experience. Let's take a closer look at this encounter. Here, we meet the commander of the invisible army of heaven, who has come to teach Joshua and us a very important lesson. Joshua was face to face with Jericho, the walled city. What strategy should he adopt to be successful? As he went out on his prayer walk, he saw a man with his sword drawn. His mission was obvious, but on which side was he deployed?

"Are you a friend or foe," Joshua asked him.

And his response was, "neither."

He comes as the commander of the army of the LORD to engage in a looming battle, and he declares that he is neutral.

And what exactly does that mean? It is an eye-opener.

The commander is there to ensure that the purposes of God Almighty are fulfilled. Fight on the side of God, and you will be fighting with the help of the commander. Disobey God and follow your own ideas, and the commander will be against you. It is as simple as that.

Having said that, the commander tells Joshua what God told Moses in the burning bush experience: "You can never go wrong with holiness, reverence, and humility before God."

This lesson is basic, particularly for us who, as kings and priests unto God, are positioned to fight the Lord's battles on earth. If we say we are deployed on the Lord's side, then we must be in the daily pursuit of obedience, holiness, reverence, and humility before God.

Nobody can say, "God is on my side: whatever I do or don't do, God is always on my side." That amounts to presumption.

No, God is neutral because He is on His side. God is on your side when you are on His side. That's the revelation. So, you make up your mind and say, "By the grace of God, from today, I will be on God's side always. I will be a remnant. I will be one of those people, righteous men, and women that Abraham was praying about so that in this our nation, whatever happens, come rain come shine, God will find me standing on His side."

That is the only way to be kings and priests unto God on earth. No matter what is happening, we fight on the Lord's side with His wisdom and might, following Him obediently every step of the way. From here we learn the big deal of living in God's presence as a priest and carrying out heaven's orders as a king. This is the obedience that releases the anointing. And that's what spiritual governance is all about.

- But first, we must be born again so that the blood of Jesus can wash away our sins and make us kings and priests unto God.
- Secondly, through faith and loving obedience to God, we rise to become friends of God who walk daily in God's will so that we can enjoy God's abiding presence.
- Thirdly, and for strategy, we always wait to be led by the Spirit of God so we can deploy on the same side as the armies of heaven, no matter the conflict.

I want to say to everyone reading this, "You are included. You can become a king and a priest unto God."

CHAPTER 11

DIVINE CHARTER
OF INCLUSION

Acts 10:34-35 (NRSV)

³⁴ Then Peter began to speak to them: "I truly understand that God shows no partiality, 35 but in every nation anyone who fears him and does what is right is acceptable to him.

The Apostle Peter came to this conclusion because a Gentile unbeliever received an angelic visitation from God because he worshipped the true God. That was bewildering to a Jew, but that spells out this Charter of Inclusion: Whosoever will, may come.

But what does it really mean that God is no respecter of persons and shows no partiality? You and I need to understand it to savor this inclusion. It should be part of our walk of faith before God. Inclusion is a big deal. It's like a title deed.

- The first thing to note is that Jehovah is not the God of the Jews only but of the Gentiles as well.

- In every nation means that all nations on this earth can benefit from the wonders of God's grace and mercy revealed through Christ. The testimony of inclusion is seen in **Revelation 7:9-10 (NRSV)** [9] After this I looked, and there was a great multitude that no one could count, from every nation, from all tribes and peoples and languages, standing before the throne and before the Lamb, robed in white, with palm branches in their hands. [10] They cried out in a loud voice, saying, "Salvation belongs to our God who is seated on the throne and to the Lamb!"

- Inclusion stands as a pillar because all have sinned and come short of the glory of God (Romans. 3:23). There are sinners in need of salvation in every nation under the sun.

- The LORD God Almighty is righteous in all His ways and holy in all His works and so provides salvation to all who repent of their sins and come to Christ for the salvation of their souls. There is no unrighteousness in God (Psalm 92:15).

- When men think God is impartial, it serves to justify the LORD as the judge who renders to every man according to his works because all the hidden things are before Him. In our ignorance, we may endorse what our God would never endorse because of His privilege of omniscience, the God who sees and knows all things.

- Whosoever fears God and does what is right is accepted before Him. That is the qualification needed by all, whether they be rich or poor, high or low, religious, moral or spiritual. The LORD is righteous, and He loves righteousness (Psalm 11:7).

The Righteous are Blessed
Matthew 5:6 (NKJV)

⁶ Blessed are those who hunger and thirst for righteousness, For they shall be filled.

No matter where we live on the surface of this earth, hunger and thirst for righteousness will open the door for the goodness and mercy of God to overtake us in our world. The God we serve is righteous. He loves righteousness, and He also loves the righteous. It is in our best interest as individuals and nations to pursue righteousness

Corruption and evil are pervasive in the world. It is not unique to any nation. The difference between nations is that in many developing nations, corruption is practiced with impunity, with no fear of consequences. In other nations, corruption is also endemic but the difference is that once the corrupt are caught, the system has a way to punish them and make them examples of what not to do. The corrupt in these nations are clever and well-connected and must keep their nefarious activities secret. In these nations it is about not being caught, not about not doing evil.

That underscores the fact that human nature is the same all over the world. Only our Lord Jesus Christ was sinless.

Kings and Priests and Righteousness

The prayer of a righteous man is powerful and effective. This is the message of the Apostle James (James 5:16b). As kings and priests unto God, we constantly make prayer decrees. If we fail to live righteously, our prayer decrees will be ineffective. So, the challenge is to resist temptation and trust God to keep us daily by the power of His Holy Spirit so we can fulfill our commission.

This bears repeating many times over. Righteousness can be a lonely road, as it was for Noah in his generation.

Genesis 7:1 (NRSV)

[1] Then the LORD said to Noah, "Go into the ark, you and all your household, for I have seen that you alone are righteous before me in this generation.

Whether we walk alone or we have others joining us, we must persevere because one righteous person can make all the difference that is needed, as we are told by the Prophet Ezekiel:

Ezekiel 22:29-30 (NLT2)

[29] Even common people oppress the poor, rob the needy, and deprive foreigners of justice. 30 "I looked for someone who might rebuild the wall of righteousness that guards the land. I searched for someone to stand in the gap in the wall so I wouldn't have to destroy the land, but I found no one.

Objective Driven Prayers

Now and again, we have objectives that help drive the passion to see things through. When we began our prayer decrees in 2017, we were led to pray for a new Nigeria in the hands of the LORD God Almighty. Later, we heard about the prophecy of the Late Pastor S. G. Elton, and we realized that we were on the same page with him. He gave a message of hope to those looking for a new Nigeria in the hands of the LORD.

- **The season of stinking corruption will be followed by a season of righteousness that will so transform us and our nation that we shall become a delightsome land.**

That is a message of hope—a message of great hope. It gives a future that confirms that the God we serve always responds to hunger and thirst after righteousness.

We must not despair, for the Scriptures tell us that God is with the generation of the righteous (Psalm 14:5). That is the story of Noah and Abraham, Isaac and Jacob. That is the story of King David. The LORD God Almighty delivered him from every attempt that King Saul made to eliminate him (2 Samuel 22:18-25). David revealed that he understood the ways of God, who said in

Deuteronomy 32:35 (NRSV):

35Vengeance is mine, and recompense, for the time when their foot shall slip; because the day of their calamity is at hand, their doom comes swiftly.

He left the judgment and punishment of King Saul in the hands of God.

In doing that, King David was ahead of his time, as we see in

Romans 12:19-21 (NKJV):

19Beloved, do not avenge yourselves, but rather give place to wrath; for it is written, "Vengeance is Mine, I will repay," says the Lord. 20Therefore "If your enemy is hungry, feed him; If he is thirsty, give him a drink; For in so doing you will heap coals of fire on his head." 21Do not be overcome by evil, but overcome evil with good.

An Oasis of Safety around the Righteous
Ezekiel 14:12-20 (NKJV)

12The word of the LORD came again to me, saying:

¹³"Son of man, when a land sins against Me by persistent unfaithfulness, I will stretch out My hand against it; I will cut off its supply of bread, send famine on it, and cut off man and beast from it. ¹⁴Even if these three men, Noah, Daniel, and Job, were in it, they would deliver only themselves by their righteousness," says the Lord GOD. ¹⁵"If I cause wild beasts to pass through the land, and they empty it, and make it so desolate that no man may pass through because of the beasts,

¹⁶even though these three men were in it, as I live," says the Lord GOD, "they would deliver neither sons nor daughters; only they would be delivered, and the land would be desolate. ¹⁷"Or if I bring a sword on that land, and say, 'Sword, go through the land,' and I cut off man and beast from it,

¹⁸even though these three men were in it, as I live," says the Lord GOD, "they would deliver neither sons nor daughters, but only they themselves would be delivered.

¹⁹"Or if I send a pestilence into that land and pour out My fury on it in blood, and cut off from it man and beast, ²⁰even though Noah, Daniel, and Job were in it, as I live," says the Lord GOD, "they would deliver neither son nor daughter; they would deliver only themselves by their righteousness."

The righteous individual has great power before God. You and I should aspire to that. Let us not be confused by the world's definition of success. There is no greater success than a life of righteousness lived before God.

1 Peter 3:12 (NRSV)

¹²For the eyes of the Lord are on the righteous, and his ears are open to their prayer. But the face of the Lord is against those who do evil."

The Prayer of a Righteous Man
James 5:16-18 (NKJV)

16Confess your trespasses to one another, and pray for one another, that you may be healed. The effective, fervent prayer of a righteous man avails much. 17Elijah was a man with a nature like ours, and he prayed earnestly that it would not rain; and it did not rain on the land for three years and six months. 18And he prayed again, and the heav en gave rain, and the earth produced its fruit.

A righteous person has power with God, particularly when he prays.

God Favors the Righteous
Hosea 2:19-22 (NKJV)

19"I will betroth you to Me forever; Yes, I will betroth you to Me In righteousness and justice, In lovingkindness and mercy; 0I will betroth you to Me in faithfulness, And you shall know the LORD. 21"It shall come to pass in that day That I will answer," says the LORD; "I will answer the heavens, And they shall answer the earth. 22The earth shall answer With grain, With new wine, And with oil; They shall answer Jezreel.

One of the greatest favors is answered prayers that bring untold blessings into our lives.

Righteousness, What Do We Mean?
Deuteronomy 6:23-25 (NKJV)

23Then He brought us out from there, that He might bring us in, to give us the land of which He swore to our fathers. 24 And the LORD commanded us to observe all these statutes, to fear the LORD our God, for our good always, that He might preserve us alive, as it is this day. 25 Then it will be righteousness for us if we are careful to observe all these commandments before the LORD our God, as He has commanded us.'

It is when we walk in God's ways, obey His commands, and simply do as He said in His Word, written or spoken to our hearts, that we become righteous before Him. There is no confusion with the imputed righteousness of Christ by which we appear before God.

Our daily walk before God in righteousness is our obligation because we have received Christ's righteousness. We live His life of righteousness because He took away our sins (2 Corinthians 5:14-15).

Hunger and Thirst for the God of Righteousness
Psalm 42:1-2 (NKJV)

¹As the deer pants for the water brooks, So pants my soul for You, O God. ² My soul thirsts for God, for the living God. When shall I come and appear before God?

When our life is centered on God, we thirst for God in every area of life, to be instructed and guided by Him so we can fulfill our purpose and destiny on earth.

Psalm 63:1-8 (NKJV)

¹O God, You are my God; Early will I seek You; My soul thirsts for You; My flesh longs for You In a dry and thirsty land Where there is no water. ²So I have looked for You in the sanctuary, To see Your power and Your glory. ³Because Your lovingkindness is better than life, My lips shall praise You.
⁴ Thus I will bless You while I live; I will lift up my hands in Your name. ⁵My soul shall be satisfied as with marrow and fatness, And my mouth shall praise You with joyful lips. ⁶When I remember You on my bed, I meditate on You in the night watches. ⁷ Because You have been my help, Therefore in the shadow of

Your wings I will rejoice. ⁸My soul follows close behind You; Your right hand upholds me.

Hunger and thirst are recognizable natural desires. But this is no ordinary hunger and also no ordinary thirst. Our Lord Jesus was speaking about the hunger of a person about to starve to death and the thirst of a person about to die of thirst as in the desert. Hunger and thirst for righteousness always open doors in heaven to bring God's favor down into our lives and our world.

- Those who hunger and thirst for righteousness always stay away from evil no matter the cost and no matter the pressure. Their sacrifices and sufferings are very precious before God.

They Shall Be Satisfied

This is the promise of the Father, that those who hunger and thirst after righteousness will be satisfied, for God will arise to endorse and justify their mission to establish righteousness in their world.

Psalm 90:14-17 (NKJV)

¹⁴Oh, satisfy us early with Your mercy, That we may rejoice and be glad all our days! ¹⁵Make us glad according to the days in which You have afflicted us, The years in which we have seen evil. ¹⁶ Let Your work appear to Your servants And Your glory to their children. ¹⁷ And let the beauty of the LORD our God be upon us, And establish the work of our hands for us; Yes, establish the work of our hands.

This is our prayer, 'Satisfy us early, O LORD our God.'

Ask, and you shall receive; seek, and you shall find; knock, and the door shall be opened unto you.

Conclusion – Encouragement
Isaiah 40:1-5 (NKJV)

[1]"Comfort, yes, comfort My people!" Says your God. [2]"Speak comfort to Jerusalem, and cry out to her, That her warfare is ended, That her iniquity is pardoned; For she has received from the LORD'S hand Double for all her sins." [3]The voice of one crying in the wilderness: "Prepare the way of the LORD; Make straight in the desert A highway for our God. [4]Every valley shall be exalted And every mountain and hill brought low; The crooked places shall be made straight And the rough places smooth; [5]The glory of the LORD shall be revealed, And all flesh shall see it together; For the mouth of the LORD has spoken."

Only the righteous can have hope in the LORD. Let us rise as individuals to pursue righteousness in our lives, our work, and our ways. Our God will come, and He will not delay. The season of righteousness is here by the finger of God, Amen. Alleluia.

CHAPTER 12

WALKING IN POWER

Mark 9:1 (ISV)

¹ Then he said to them, "Truly I tell you, some people standing here will not experience death until they see the kingdom of God arrive with power."

In the above passage, our Lord Jesus was looking forward to the Day of Pentecost when the Holy Spirit came down, and the Church of God was born in power. Several waves of the Holy Spirit visitation have come to different parts of the world ever since, to establish the Kingdom of God in the lives of men and women on earth with power.

These waves of Holy Spirit visitations have made us understand that what our Lord had said here went beyond Pentecost. Generations of kings and priests unto God can arise and desire to see the Kingdom of God come with power in their lifetime. This is the real challenge before us in this generation. We must not be satisfied with organized religion and its rituals. We must thirst for the outpouring of the Spirit to see men and women come under conviction and conversion and rise to lead new lives of godliness that impact their world for God and to the benefit of men.

If men and women in bygone generations can desire to see the Kingdom of God come with power in their lifetime, why not us in this generation? God is no respecter of persons and so He will answer anyone and everyone who hunger and thirst to see the Kingdom of God come with power. The ball is in our court.

The early disciples understood the place of power for kings and priests unto God. They waited in Jerusalem for the Holy Ghost to arrive, just like they were instructed to do by our Lord Jesus. What they experienced on the day of Pentecost was so explosive that it revolutionized their thinking about themselves and their calling to bring the Kingdom of God to men and women on earth. Their experience cured them of all timidity and diffidence and threw them out onto the streets to challenge the status quo. It was the same assurance of power that cured Moses of his timidity and feelings of inadequacy:

Exodus 3:11-12 (NRSV)

[11] But Moses said to God, "Who am I that I should go to Pharaoh, and bring the Israelites out of Egypt?" [12] He said, "I will be with you; and this shall be the sign for you that it is I who sent you: when you have brought the people out of Egypt, you shall worship God on this mountain."

Kings and Priests need Power

Kings and priests unto God in every generation must be empowered to carry out the same commission. But we must understand the power that came down. He is the Holy Spirit. He is not a phenomenon or an effect. He is the third person in the Trinity with a mandate to produce in us and through us the agenda of heaven, which is men and women who are like Christ (Romans 8:29).

Pentecostal Power

The impression often given is that the Holy Spirit's presence is only about signs and wonders. Signs and wonders advertise the ministry of the Holy Spirit, but what He did on the day of Pentecost was to bring conviction and conversion to 3000 souls who were brought into the Kingdom of God. Men and women who encounter the Holy Spirit on the day of their conversion know what the encounter did in them, for them, and through them.

I was going away from the meeting hall that fateful Sunday, June 28, 1970, without giving my life to Christ. Less than a hundred meters from the hall, I heard a voice that said to me, "Go and write your name down. That is where you belong. You don't belong to where you are going." I thought someone was behind me. When I turned and saw nobody, I went and wrote my name down as a new convert to Christ as instructed, not sure what it was all about. But that night, as I slept, a voice said to me in a dream: "Get up and read John 6:20." That Scripture says, "It is I be not afraid." That was it. My journey of commitment to Christ had begun.

When we come to Christ under conviction, the same Holy Spirit who brought us in will also keep us until we see our Lord Jesus in glory.

Miracles, Signs, and Wonders

These are the advertising tools of the Holy Spirit to bring men and women to Christ. He used it powerfully when the cripple that everyone knew was healed at the Beautiful Gate of the temple in Jerusalem. It gave opportunity to the disciples to expound the mysteries of Christ.

Acts 3:16 (NKJV)

[16] And His name, through faith in His name, has made this man strong, whom you see and know. Yes, the faith which comes through Him has given him this perfect soundness in the presence of you all.

The miracle was the advert, but the goal was to bring men and women into the Kingdom of God under the anointing.

Acts 3:19 (NKJV)

[19] Repent therefore and be converted, that your sins may be blotted out, so that times of refreshing may come from the presence of the Lord,

That goal was powerfully met on that day as about five thousand believed and were saved:

Acts 4:4 (NKJV)

[4] However, many of those who heard the word believed, and the number of the men came to be about five thousand.

We must note the Word they heard after they saw the miracle:

Acts 3:26 (NKJV)

²⁶ *To you first, God, having raised up His Servant Jesus, sent Him to bless you, in turning away every one of you from your iniquities."*

The Holy Spirit used the miracle to bring the people so they could hear that God wants each of us to repent and turn away from our sins. The Apostles knew this and preached it. Miracles are not the end but the tool to bring men and women to God so that their lives can be completely transformed.

But miracles are necessary to the Gospel message as tools for conveying God's mercy and compassion for suffering humanity so that men and women can come to God and be saved from their sins. Nothing in the Bible or from experience suggests that miracles have ceased.

I needed a miracle in 1974 to be able to anchor one evening of the mission to the University of Ibadan, organized by the Ibadan Varsity Christian Union. I had turned down the invitation because I was very sick. After I turned it down, it triggered a conversation with the Holy Spirit. He asked me a question in my heart:

"Do you believe that God knows everything?"

"Yes, I do," was my prompt response.

"That means He must know that you will be sick today?"

"Yes, of course," I responded.

"And despite knowing that you will be sick, He led the organizers of this meeting to invite you to anchor this one night?"

"Yes!"

That set me thinking and wondering.

Then He said to me, "In that case, you must anchor the meeting."

That was it. I went to the auditorium weak, feeble, and very chesty. But the moment I picked up the microphone, a vibration went through me, and I was instantly made whole. Strength and energy flooded into me miraculously, and everything was normal again.

I believe in miracles, and I have received quite a few in my life. I was a Senior Resident at the Lagos University Teaching Hospital when this happened, between 1983 and 1985. Without warning, I began to have pain in my back in the early evening. I prayed and went to bed. The pain woke me up in the middle of the night. I remember it clearly as if it were yesterday. We were living on the second floor in one of the staff quarters. I got out of bed and decided to go out into the open to pray.

As I went down the stairs, I said to God, "LORD, between You, myself and the devil, I am not afraid."

The Holy Spirit whispered back to me, "Son, there is nothing wrong with you."

"Nothing wrong with me?" I reached my hand to the location of the pain, which had become somewhat excruciating. Then suddenly, it got to me that word of faith: "There's nothing wrong with me." Then I burst out laughing at about 4 am in the morning. "Devil, you are a liar. There is nothing wrong with me. As I laughed, the pain went away like something being deflated. And I was completely pain-free. I have never had it again ever since, and I dare say, never will in the name of Jesus, Amen.

My journey of faith and miracles began in earnest when I was led by the Holy Spirit to make God my primary care physician. Not sure what year it was. That decision meant that if I felt ill, I must first report to God before I report to man. I always follow His leading in seeking medical help. After I turned 70, I felt ill and was admitted to the intensive care unit of a hospital for eight days. As I lay on that bed ill, I began to thank God that He kept me for 70 years without ever seeing the inside of a hospital as a patient. Three days after I was discharged from intensive care, I was on my way home. All glory to God.

The Fruit of the Holy Spirit

Transforming a life can be hard and frustrating. But the Father's goal in sending His Son, our Lord Jesus, to the world is to raise men and women who are conformed to the character of the Son, Christ (Romans 8:29).

Each of us, as kings and priests unto God, must allow the Holy Spirit to accomplish this work in us. The Bible tells us that as we behold our Lord Jesus and the life He lived while He was here, we will be transformed into the same image.

2 Corinthians 3:18 (NRSV)

[18] And all of us, with unveiled faces, seeing the glory of the Lord as though reflected in a mirror, are being transformed into the same image from one degree of glory to another; for this comes from the Lord, the Spirit.

The Fruit of the Spirit is Christ's character unveiled. As we behold Him live out each component fruit in the Bible, we are changed when we allow the Holy Spirit to manifest His life through us. For this reason, we can say that manifesting the Fruit of the Spirit involves obedience to the leadership of the Holy Spirit in our lives. When we respond as He tells us, we manifest the fruit needed in our situation.

Galatians 5:22-23 (NRSV)

22 By contrast, the fruit of the Spirit is love, joy, peace, patience, kindness, generosity, faithfulness, 23 gentleness, and self-control. There is no law against such things.

What the Holy Spirit does is orchestrate circumstances in our lives as kings and priests that will teach us all nine of these dimensions of the Fruit of the Spirit in very practical ways. Our Lord Jesus passed through the same process we are told in

Hebrews 5:7-10 (NRSV)

7 In the days of his flesh, Jesus offered up prayers and supplications, with loud cries and tears, to the one who was able to save him from death, and he was heard because of his reverent submission. 8 Although he was a Son, he learned obedience through what he suffered; 9 and having been made perfect, he became the source of eternal salvation for all who obey him, 10 having been designated by God a high priest according to the order of Melchizedek.

He struggled with the ordeal of the Cross, and it all came to a head in the Garden of Gethsemane, where He submitted to the will of God. If our high priest went through this process, we all, as kings and priests under Him, must submit to it for our good, so that we may fulfill our destiny individually the way He did.

The Gifts of the Holy Spirit

We are told to desire the Gifts of the Holy Spirit so that the Church may be edified or built up. We are also told to desire the best gifts. The gifts are generally divided into three groups.

- The Word of Wisdom, the Word of Knowledge, and the Discernment of Spirits are often referred to as Revelation Gifts because they bring knowledge and insight in a supernatural way.
- The gift of Faith, Diverse Gifts of Healing, and the Working of Miracles are called Power Gifts.
- The Gift of Prophecy, Diverse Tongues, and the Interpretation of Tongues are called Gifts of Inspiration

What is important for every king and priest is to understand these gifts and desire them whenever or wherever they are needed. The fact that they are gifts means that everyone can desire and receive them to fulfill God's purposes for their lives.

In Acts chapter 5, Ananias and Sapphira, his wife, lied to the Apostles. Through the Word of Knowledge, their lie was revealed to the Apostle Peter. The judgment that followed put the fear of God in the young Church. This may sound drastic, but the judgment of heaven is beyond us. That fear of God so early in the life of the Church must have been badly needed.

The Spirit of Consecration and Sanctification

Our Lord Jesus prayed that we should be separated from the world and also be sanctified by the truth.

John 17:15-17 (NRSV)

15 I am not asking you to take them out of the world, but I ask you to protect them from the evil one. 16 They do not belong to the world, just as I do not belong to the world. 17 Sanctify them in the truth; your word is truth.

There is a spirit in the world from which kings and priests must be separated. That spirit does not have godly values and is ready to compromise with evil. It is often focused on the organization rather than on the Kingdom of God. It thrives on competition rather than cooperation. It does not often understand self-sacrificing love. It can be ego-driven and pays no attention to the will of God and the glory of God.

The Apostle John's first letter admonished us in

1 John 2:15-17 (NRSV)

15 Do not love the world or the things in the world. The love of the Father is not in those who love the world; 16 for all that is in the world—the desire of the flesh, the desire of the eyes, the pride in riches—comes not from the Father but from the world. 17 And the world and its desire are passing away, but those who do the will of God live forever.

When we love the world, we grieve the Holy Spirit, who hates to compete with the world for our love, obedience, and loyalty. The Apostle James pointed that out to us.

James 4:4-5 (NLT2)

4 You adulterers! Don't you realize that friendship with the world makes you an enemy of God? I say it again: If you want to be a friend of the world, you make yourself an enemy of God.
5 What do you think the Scriptures mean when they say that the spirit God has placed within us is filled with envy?

The last thing you want in your life is to provoke divine jealousy. His jealousy burns like a blazing fire (SS 8:6).

We never forget that the God of love is also a consuming fire (Hebrews 12:29).

Strength to Love

Our Lord Jesus Christ is the King who rules by love. His way is to love men and women to submission. He does not compel or coerce. Through His love, He compels us to live His life on the earth. The Apostle Paul testified to this in

2 Corinthians 5:14-15 (NIV)

14 For Christ's love compels us because we are convinced that one died for all, and therefore all died. 15 And he died for all that those who live should no longer live for themselves but for him who died for them and was raised again.

The love of God is poured into our hearts by the Holy Spirit (Romans 5:5). The strength to love like our Lord Jesus Christ is given to us by the Holy Spirit (Ephesians 3:14-16). A simple prayer, when followed by obedience to the Holy Spirit, will enlarge our capacity for self-sacrificing love.

When we grow in the expression of the love of Christ, the nature of God is implanted in us (Ephesians 3:17-19).

Love Begets Power with God

We are admonished to be strong in the Lord and in the power of His might (Ephesians 6:10). Many wonder how that can be done. Our Lord Jesus told us that God's presence would be with us if we love and obey Him (John 14:23). Besides, faith is energized by love as we are told (Galatians 5:6). The more we love and obey God, the more we trust Him and the more we trust Him, the more He honors our faith in Him. (Hebrews 11:6).

This is not a religious calling. As kings and priests unto God, we build a deep bond of love with God through loyalty, love, and obedience.

KINGS AND PRIESTS WALKING IN POWER AND AUTHORITY

Our Lord Jesus told the seventy after they returned from the mission trip in

Luke 10:17-20 (NKJV).

17 Then the seventy returned with joy, saying, "Lord, even the demons are subject to us in Your name." 18And He said to them, "I saw Satan fall like lightning from heaven. 19Behold, I give you the authority to trample on serpents and scorpions, and over all the power of the enemy, and nothing shall by any means hurt you. 20Nevertheless do not rejoice in this, that the spirits are subject to you, but rather rejoice because your names are written in heaven."

Spiritual power is required to actualize the agenda of the Kingdom of God Almighty and His Christ. When God commissioned Moses, He said to him, "I will be with you." When He commissioned Gideon to dislodge the Midianites, He said to him, "I will be with you." When our Lord Jesus commissioned the eleven disciples, He told them to wait for the power from on high before they began. The power needed to actualize the agenda of the Kingdom of Heaven on earth is the power of the Holy Spirit. Everything about spiritual power must revolve around a dynamic relationship with the Holy Spirit. Three things are needed for this:

- Guidance through the Word and through Communion
- The Anointing
- Holiness and sanctification

The power of the Holy Spirit is not magic. It is based on a dynamic relationship of love and obedience, the pursuit of the divine will and agenda, holiness, and loyalty to God. He comes into our lives to empower us to live a life of self-sacrificing love and holiness so we can become God's habitation on earth (Ephesians 2:22).

The mission of the Holy Spirit is to

- Bring conviction and conversion into the hearts of men and women so that they may be saved.
- Empower men and women to conform to the image of Christ so they can live the life of Christ in their world - at home, at work, at business in society, and in the Church.
- Sanctify us daily through the Word of God so we can become and remain vessels of honor to our God every day of our lives (2 Timothy 2:19-21).
- Minister to our world through us by His power at work within us to manifest God's plans and purposes in time so that glory may come to God through us (Ephesians 3:20-21).

We must always remember that spiritual governance is impossible without the Holy Spirit. He is the One who, with His power, actualizes our decrees.

Let us note that any and every king and priest can be empowered. When we fast and pray, it is to secure a season of quiet before the LORD so we can hear Him more readily and be more sensitive to the communion of the Holy Spirit.

How can we walk in power on the earth in our lives? Here is the power arrangement made for us explained to us by no other than our Lord Jesus Christ Himself in

Luke 10:17-20 (NKJV).

[17] Then the seventy returned with joy, saying, "Lord, even the demons are subject to us in Your name." 18And He said to them, "I saw Satan fall like lightning from heaven. 19Behold, I give you the authority to trample on serpents and scorpions, and over all the power of the enemy, and nothing shall by any means hurt you. 20Nevertheless do not rejoice in this, that the spirits are subject to you, but rather rejoice because your names are written in heaven."

The seventy returned from their missionary journey excited by the success of their mission. The success was that demons were subject to them in Jesus' name. Wow! Our Lord Jesus explained what happened. Satan was dislodged, and he tumbled to the earth in a flash. Now, going forward, our Lord Jesus said, I give you authority or *exousia* to tread on serpents and scorpions, and over all the power or *dunamis* of the enemy, and nothing shall by any means *hurt you*. Now, here is the way the arrangement works. *Authority gives the order, and the power enforces it.*

When we give the order, where is the power to carry it out?

We go to **John 14:15-17 (NKJV)** to discover the power arrangement that our Lord Jesus made for us.

15 "If you love Me, keep My commandments. 16And I will pray the Father, and He will give you another Helper, that He may abide with you forever— 17the Spirit of truth, whom the world cannot receive, because it neither sees Him nor knows Him; but you know Him, for He dwells with you and will be in you.

- If you love me and keep my commandments, the Holy Spirit will come and live inside you.
- When the Holy Spirit lives inside, the power source has come inside. The power will be at work from within us.

The Apostle Paul explained this in **Ephesians 3:20-21 (NKJV):**

20Now to Him who is able to do exceedingly abundantly above all that we ask or think, according to the power that works in us, 21to Him be glory in the church by Christ Jesus to all generations, forever and ever. Amen.

The reason why the Holy Spirit is coming to dwell within us is to: Restore the divinity within our humanity exactly the way it was with Christ.

Matthew 3:16 (NKJV)

16 When He had been baptized, Jesus came up immediately from the water; and behold, the heavens were opened to Him, and He saw the Spirit of God descending like a dove and alighting upon Him.

Notice that the moment the Holy Spirit came upon Him, He took over His program completely.

Luke 4:1-2 (NKJV)

¹Then Jesus, being filled with the Holy Spirit, returned from the Jordan and was led by the Spirit into the wilderness, ²being tempted for forty days by the devil. And in those days He ate nothing, and afterward, when they had ended, He was hungry.

Notice again what happened after the temptation in **Luke 4:14-18 (NKJV).**

¹⁴Then Jesus returned in the power of the Spirit to Galilee, and news of Him went out through all the surrounding region. ¹⁵And He taught in their synagogues, being glorified by all. ¹⁶So He came to Nazareth, where He had been brought up. And as His custom was, He went into the synagogue on the Sabbath day, and stood up to read. ¹⁷And He was handed the book of the prophet Isaiah. And when He had opened the book, He found the place where it was written: ¹⁸"The Spirit of the LORD is upon Me, Because He has anointed Me To preach the gospel to the poor; He has sent Me to heal the brokenhearted, To proclaim liberty to the captives And recovery of sight to the blind, To set at liberty those who are oppressed;

Notice that He did not lose the presence of the Spirit during His wilderness temptation. That is how we learn not to lose the anointing on our lives during temptation. Instead, our Lord Jesus came from the temptation full of the Holy Spirit after defeating the devil on the three major counts of:

- The lust of the flesh – bread.
- The lust of the eyes – ambition revealed as wealth or what we call fame and fortune.
- The pride of life – false faith that said, jump and angels will catch You and the world will hail You as the new sensation in town.

Our Lord Jesus returned from the temptation in the power of the Spirit. Now here is a prayer. Say it with me:

- "LORD, in every hour of temptation, may I not lose the anointing on my life. But instead, may I come out of every temptation in the power of the Holy Spirit just like my Lord and Master, that I may be and do all that You have called me to be and do on earth, in Jesus' name, Amen.

May every temptation make you and I stronger in the Lord and in the power of His might in Jesus' name, Amen.

Spiritual Empowerment

God Almighty spoke once, and twice I heard it, that power belongs to God. Power is exclusive to God. All *dunamis* belong to God. When God created the angels, He gave them power in quanta, according to their level. That is why angels are in hierarchies as angels, and archangels. We do not know more than that about angels. Some of these angels are so powerful that they can deal with Satan any time God Almighty gives the order.

Come with me to Revelation 9:1 (GW):

¹When the fifth angel blew his trumpet, I saw a star that had fallen to earth from the sky. The star was given the key to the shaft of the bottomless pit.

The star is a very powerful angel that we see again in **Revelation 20:1-3 (GW):**

¹I saw an angel coming down from heaven, holding the key to the bottomless pit and a large chain in his hand. ²He overpowered the serpent, that ancient snake, named Devil and Satan. The angel chained up the serpent for 1,000 years. ³He threw it into the bottomless pit. The angel shut and sealed the pit over the serpent to keep it from deceiving the nations anymore until the 1,000 years were over. After that, it must be set free for a little while.

Here is another prayer you and I must pray now:

- Father, I thank You that in Your power arrangement in this world, You made provision for me to walk in power. Grant me the grace to walk daily in Your power, knowing that the hosts of heaven under You are there to minister to me as I pursue Your Kingdom and Your glory on the earth in the name of Jesus. Amen.

The Bible tells us that there are elemental spirits, principalities, powers, rulers of the darkness of this world, and spiritual wickedness in high places.

Our Lord Jesus went frequently before the Father for instruction and empowerment as the Son of Man and so must we. Two examples suffice:

Mark 1:35 (NKJV)

[35]Now in the morning, having risen a long while before daylight, He went out and departed to a solitary place; and there He prayed.

Here is another in **Luke 18:1 (KJV).**

[1]And he spake a parable unto them to this end, that men ought always to pray, and not to faint;

When Joshua, the high priest, came before God for empowerment (Zechariah 3:1-9), a serious hindrance was revealed. Joshua was covered with filthy garments, and the devil was standing by his right hand to resist him. How can someone stand at your right hand and yet resist you? When we say someone is my right-hand man, we mean the person is with me on the journey of life. He is someone I trust to walk with me on the way. But this righthand man was resisting Joshua instead of helping him. That calls for caution for all of us to be wary of false bits of help who pretend to help but actually hinder our spiritual journey through temptations and sin.

Three sources of temptation around us are the flesh, the world, and the devil. These are hindrances to our empowerment. They are standing with us, but they are there to hinder us rather than to promote the Kingdom of God in our lives. So let us always watch out for the influences of the flesh, the world, and the devil. They are there to hinder rather than to help.

James 4:4-6 (NLT2)

⁴You adulterers and adulteresses! Don't you realize that friendship with the world makes you an enemy of God? I say it again: If you want to be a friend of the world, you make yourself an enemy of God. ⁵What do you think the Scriptures mean when they say that the spirit God has placed within us is filled with envy? ⁶But he gives us even more grace to stand against such evil desires. As the Scriptures say, **"God opposes the proud but favors the humble."**

The first thing Joshua needed before empowerment was cleansing by sovereign grace. This is revealed in **Zechariah 3:3-4:**

³Joshua was standing there, wearing filthy clothes.
⁴The angel said to his heavenly attendants, "Take away the filthy clothes this man is wearing." Then he said to Joshua, "I have taken away your sin and will give you new clothes to wear."

- There is always cleansing before empowerment. No cleansing, no empowerment.

The prophet Isaiah had cleansing before empowerment in (Isaiah 6:5-9**).**

After Joshua the high priest was cleansed, he was ready for empowerment. (Zechariah 3:5-8)

- Notice that empowered saints are the hope of a good future when the Branch, our Lord Jesus Christ arrives on the scene.

Zechariah 3:8: (TEV)

⁸Listen then, Joshua, you who are the High Priest; and listen, you fellow priests of his, you that are the sign of a good future: I will reveal my servant, who is called The Branch!

But what will the Branch do when He comes? The answer is revealed in **1 John 2:12 (GW).**

¹²I'm writing to you, dear children, because your sins are forgiven through Christ.

The cleansing that Joshua and Isaiah received through sovereign grace is now available to us through the blood of our Lord and savior Jesus Christ. Alleluia!

Finally, let us always remember that we need to be empowered. Therefore, we must appear often before God's holy presence for empowerment.

We have advice from King David in **Psalm 55:17-18 (NLT2)**

¹⁷ Morning, noon, and night I cry out in my distress, and the LORD hears my voice. 18 He ransoms me and keeps me safe from the battle waged against me, though many still oppose me.

Accessing God's Presence

The first thing we do when we pray is to cleanse ourselves in the Blood of Jesus (Hebrews 10:19-21).

There is always some filthiness that needs to be cleansed, as revealed in this Scripture:

2 Corinthians 7:1 (GW).

¹ Since we have these promises, dear friends, we need to cleanse ourselves from everything that contaminates body and spirit and live a holy life in the fear of God.

Filthiness of flesh and spirit abound in thought, word and deed and none of them can enter God's holy presence.

- When we cleanse ourselves in the blood of Jesus, we are made holy, unblameable and irreproachable and so appear before God without a single fault (Colossians 1:21-22)

KINGS AND PRIESTS UNTO GOD—RECAP

Revelation 1:5-6 (NKJV)

⁵and from Jesus Christ, the faithful witness, the firstborn from the dead, and the ruler over the kings of the earth. To Him who loved us and washed us from our sins in His own blood,
⁶and has made us kings and priests to His God and Father, to Him be glory and dominion forever and ever. Amen.

This is the foundation of walking in authority and power on earth before God so that we can become the hope of a good future for our nations, no matter where we are.

Our Lord Jesus Christ is our High Priest (Hebrews 4:14-15)

His priesthood is after the order of Melchizedek (Hebrews 5:5-6)

Our priesthood is also after the order of Melchizedek because Christ is our high priest and we are priests under Him.

Melchizedek was both king and priest (Hebrews 7:1-3 (NKJV).

That is why we are called a **royal priesthood.** We are made both kings and priests unto God through Christ (1 Peter 2:9-10). The purpose of making us kings and priests or a royal priesthood is to establish the Kingdom of God in the hearts of men and women on earth.

This is what the Kingdom of God means when it is revealed in the hearts of men and women on earth – righteousness, peace and joy in the Holy Spirit (Romans 14:17).

Melchizedek was the King of righteousness and peace. As priests in the order of Melchizedek, we are empowered by God Almighty to establish righteousness, peace, and joy in the Holy Ghost in the lives of men and women on earth.

Walking in Power

This is the lesson of Zechariah 3:6-7 (TEV).

⁶Then the angel told Joshua that ⁷ the LORD Almighty had said: "If you obey my laws and perform the duties I have assigned you, then you will continue to be in charge of my Temple and its courts, and I will hear your prayers, just as I hear the prayers of the angels who are in my presence.

After cleansing we enter the holy of holies in heaven in our prayers and join the angels and the twenty-four elders to worship His holiness and majesty. There, we humble ourselves like the elders and put all notion of merit away as we bow our hearts in submission and desire His will and glory in every area of our lives. This is when we seek to be empowered so that His plans and purposes can be established in us and through us. This is something everyone of us can do and do routinely too.

To be empowered and have God answer our prayers, the Angel admonished the high priest Joshua to:

- Be faithful to His calling
- Be obedient to God's commands in His Word as well as those spoken to his heart.

This is the secret to empowerment for everybody. Our lord Jesus lived in complete obedience to the Father. He left us that example to follow.

Let's pay attention to empowerment as revealed to Joshua in Zechariah 3:7b:

- I will empower you as I empower and answer the prayers of the angels in My presence, and I will hear your prayers just as I hear the prayers of the angels who are in My presence.

This is why we join the angels in their worship and cast our crowns before Him like the elders, offering Him all that we are and all that we have for His glory in our lives. Part of worship must be a consecration and commitment to please God in our lives as our Lord Jesus revealed in **John 8:28-29 (NKJV):**

²⁸ *Then Jesus said to them, "When you lift up the Son of Man, then you will know that I am He, and that I do nothing of Myself; but as My Father taught*

Me, I speak these things. 29 And He who sent Me is with Me. The Father has not left Me alone, for I always do those things that please Him."

Our Lord Jesus said:

- I always do those things that please the Father.

That is the secret to God's abiding presence and empowerment. It makes prayer special, powerful and effective as our Lord Jesus revealed in

Mark 11:24 (NKJV)

24Therefore, I say to you, whatever things you ask when you pray, believe that you receive them, and you will have them.

Empowerment is about praying and receiving power or anointing from heaven. Our Lord Jesus taught us to ask that we may receive. When we appear before God therefore, we must ask for empowerment to do the will of God in our lives on earth. We rise from our prayers, believing we have been empowered. We go into our world knowing that God Almighty has empowered us to do His will on the earth. It is not necessary to feel empowered, even though it helps us. What matters is to know that we have been empowered and that faith will bring the anointing down - *Whatever you ask in prayer, believe you have received and you will have. Amen.*

CHAPTER 13

PRACTICING
SPIRITUAL
GOVERNANCE

Anyone who is born again and baptized in the Holy Spirit can be a spiritual governor. Our Lord Jesus told His disciples to wait in Jerusalem until the power of the Holy Spirit was released upon them. If you believe and you are yet to be baptized, then seek to be baptized. That was the way the empowered early Christians in the Bible functioned.

Acts 8:14-17 (NKJV)

14 Now when the apostles who were at Jerusalem heard that Samaria had received the word of God, they sent Peter and John to them, 15 who, when they had come down, prayed for them that they might receive the Holy Spirit. 16 For as yet He had fallen upon none of them. They had only been baptized in the name of the Lord Jesus. 17 Then they laid hands on them, and they received the Holy Spirit.

This was also the practice of Apostle Paul at Ephesus and everywhere he went, presumably.

Acts 19:1-7 (NKJV)

¹ And it happened, while Apollos was at Corinth, that Paul, having passed through the upper regions, came to Ephesus. And finding some disciples 2 he said to them, "Did you receive the Holy Spirit when you believed?" So they said to him, "We have not so much as heard whether there is a Holy Spirit." 3 And he said to them, "Into what then were you baptized?" So they said, "Into John's baptism." 4 Then Paul said, "John indeed baptized with a baptism of repentance, saying to the people that they should believe on Him who would come after him, that is, on Christ Jesus." 5 When they heard this, they were baptized in the name of the Lord Jesus. 6 And when Paul had laid hands on them, the Holy Spirit came upon them, and they spoke with tongues and prophesied. 7 Now the men were about twelve in all.

Baptism in the Holy Spirit was necessary for them to believe and know that the presence and power of the Holy Spirit were in them as they were in the early Apostles; there was no difference.

Keeping Abreast with Development

The news organs, whether they be television or newspaper, tell us what is going on in our world. Social media also lets us know what is happening in our world. Kings and priests must know what is going on in their world, particularly evil, wickedness, injustice, immorality, and stuff like pandemics, so they can make decrees to uproot them. We must not be slow to respond so that heaven will see that we are eager to establish the Kingdom of God and its righteousness on earth. This is what will make heaven send us preemptive revelations that tell us of impending disasters about to unfold in our world so we can take action.

- The LORD God Almighty said of His friend Abraham, "Shall I hide from Abraham what I am about to do in Sodom? (Genesis 18:17). In the same way, as kings and priests unto God, God will tip us off about permissions being sought and about plots being hatched by men and devils to enable us to take preemptive action. Our duty is to be available and attentive to what He is saying by communion, dreams, and revelations.

The prophet Amos tells us that God always informs us, as His prophets and priests, when things are about to happen.

Amos 3:7 (NRSV)

7 Surely the Lord God does nothing, without revealing his secret to his servants the prophets.

Also, the Bible tells us that God is looking for someone to pray and act so that calamity will not overtake a place (Ezekiel 22:29-31).

"I looked for a man to stand in the gap… that I may not destroy the place." Does this sound familiar to you? It inspired us to begin praying for a new Nigeria in the hand of the LORD. The Holy Spirit gave us prayer decrees to use daily to turn things around for our good.

- Always remember that if no one makes decrees to stop evil and reroute chaos and disaster, calamity after calamity will happen. *No prayer decrees, no response from heaven.*

- Spiritual vigilance is a must. We come before God seeking to know if there are issues that we need to be concerned about. If there are many of us asking in prayer, different challenges related to the making of a new nation will be revealed to us, enabling us to direct prayers and decrees to God to solve them.

- We must always remember that a few disciples dismantled idolatry and planted the Light of Jesus's life in their world through the exercise of spiritual governance, which multiplied their efforts. The work done in the realm of the Spirit is just as important, if not more important, than the work done in the natural realm.

- The Book of Acts provides details about when to go, where to go, how long to stay, and other such details that maximized their efforts and led them to people who became pillars in the work of planting and expanding the Kingdom of God in the lives of men and women on earth.

To move in the same vein with them, we need to gather like-minded people together, rehash the principles of spiritual governance with them, and then begin to pray and act as directed by the Holy Spirit. They can catch up on the details, but it is essential that prayer decrees go up to heaven to give God and His angels materials to act on to deliver us.

2 Corinthians 10:3-6 (NKJV)

³For though we walk in the flesh, we do not war according to the flesh. ⁴For the weapons of our warfare are not carnal but mighty in God for pulling down strongholds, ⁵casting down arguments and every high thing that exalts itself against the knowledge of God, bringing every thought into captivity to the obedience of Christ, 6and being ready to punish all disobedience when your obedience is fulfilled.

Job 22:27-30 (KJV)

27Thou shalt make thy prayer unto him, and he shall hear thee, and thou shalt pay thy vows. 28Thou shalt also decree a thing, and it shall be established unto thee: and the light shall shine upon thy ways.

29When men are cast down, then thou shalt say, There is lifting up; and he shall save the humble person.

30He shall deliver the island of the innocent: and it is delivered by the pureness of thine hands.

The Hope of a Good Nation Like Nigeria

Empowered Christians who make decrees to establish righteousness and peace in their nation (Nigeria} are the hope of a good nation (Nigeria) that will be revealed in due course. Join that company now. Glory, Alleluia!

CHAPTER 14

ADDENDUM MARCHING ORDERS AND GOVERNANCE PRAYERS

Matthew 28:18-20 (NRSV)

[18] And Jesus came and said to them, "All authority in heaven and on earth has been given to me. 19 Go therefore and make disciples of all nations, baptizing them in the name of the Father and of the Son and of the Holy Spirit, 20 and teaching them to obey everything that I have commanded you. And remember, I am with you always, to the end of the age."

The Great Commission is for everybody. Wherever you are, you can assemble a small group of like-minded believers, and you can begin to take spiritual authority in your world to spread the knowledge of God and His Christ and so establish the Kingdom of God in the hearts of men and women.

When we started governance prayers in 2017, we followed the Holy Spirit as He taught and trained us about what to do and how to do it. There is no formula for spiritual governance, but the governance prayers shared below reveal a few vital principles.

PRAYER OF ACCESS

- **We come to You ancient of days, the God of all** Heaven **and earth. We worship You, O King of all the ages, who does all things after the counsel of** Your **own will.**

- **We proceed right now to wash ourselves in the** Blood of Jesus Christ, **Your Son, and to clothe ourselves fully in His righteousness, thanking** You **for all** Your **love and mercy. We acknowledge that we are most undeserving of all** Your **love, and we are deeply grateful for** Your **kindness in accepting us in** Your **beloved.**

(Please take a moment to wash yourself in the Blood of Jesus of all filthiness of flesh and spirit and to clothe yourself fully in the Righteousness of Christ our Saviour. Hebrews 10:19-22)

- **We approach** Your **throne of grace in humility with gratitude, confessing the virtue and power in the** Blood of Your **Son Jesus Christ that has made us accepted in** Your **most holy presence. O LORD our God, we thank** You **and bless** Your **glorious name. Amen**

- Our Father **and** our God, **we come to join the four living creatures and the four and twenty elders with all the community of angels and archangels to give You glory, for You are God alone, the immortal, the invisible, the God only wise, the beginning and end of all things, the**

Ancient **of** Days, **who dwells in light unapproachable; the great** I AM that I AM.

Therefore, we come to join the heavenly hosts to sing:

Holy, holy, holy is the LORD God Almighty

Who was, and is, and is to come!

We bow our hearts in humble adoration with the four and twenty elders to say:

You are worthy, O LORD, to receive glory and honor and power

For You created all things, And by Your will and for Your pleasure, we all exist and were created

LORD, **we come to give** You **thanks and praise and worship; we come to give** You **honor, adoration, and majesty for who** You **are and for what** You **do every moment to sustain the universe and the entire creation and us here gathered by** Your **mercy.**

O Father **of grace and glory, Your will is our command as we worship** Your **majesty and holiness, singing:**

Holy, holy, holy is the LORD God Almighty

Who was and is and is to come!

May it please **You, O LORD our God,** to conform us into the image of **Your Son Jesus Christ** by **Your Spirit,** for we desire to walk this earth the same way **He** walked it, doing **Your** will the way **He** did it, with love, loyalty, and obedience, and we desire to walk daily in the fullness of **His** power and authority, just the way **He** did, to establish the **Kingdom** of God and the rule and reign of **Your Son Jesus Christ** in the hearts of all eight billion inhabitants in the 244 nations on this earth; and to dismantle all opposition of men and devils to **Your Kingdom** in every nation on earth by the resurrection power conferred upon us as **Your** saints, to the exclusive glory of **Your** Most Holy Name, in **Jesus'** matchless name we pray, Amen.

We use this prayer of access every time we gather because it contains Scriptures that teach us how to access God's presence. It is important to state that there is no formula for this. The Holy Spirit is our spiritual draughtsman and helps us put together what the Father wants to hear on each subject.

PRAYER FOR THE MAKING OF A RIGHTEOUS NIGERIA

(Anyone can use this for their nation)

As we began praying for a new Nigeria in the hand of the LORD in 2017, we were not aware that the late Pastor S. G. Elton had given a prophecy in 1978 or thereabouts. Because we are on the same page, we adopted the prophecy, which has now crystallized into the making of a Righteous Nigeria.

Actualizing Pa S.G. Elton's Prophecy - The Making of a Righteous Nigeria

Hebrews 11:3 (NKJV)

By faith we understand that the worlds were framed by the word of God, so that the things which are seen were not made of things which are visible.

Prayer

- O LORD our God, **we receive** Your **Word to us Nigerians, through Pa Elton, that our nation Nigeria will be known for corruption and that the name Nigeria will stink as a result of this corruption. But after this phase of corruption, we shall enter into the phase of righteousness when we shall be known for righteousness all over the world, and people will be coming to us from all over the world to learn the way of righteousness.**

Prayer Authorization

Hebrews 11:3 (NRSV)

3 By faith, we understand that the worlds were prepared by the word of God so that what is seen was made from things that are not visible.

Isaiah 14:24 & 27 (NKJV)

24 The LORD of hosts has sworn, saying, "Surely, as I have thought, so it shall come to pass, And as I have purposed, so it shall stand: 27 For the LORD of hosts has purposed, And who will annul it? His hand is stretched out, And who will turn it back?"

Jeremiah 29:11 (KJV)

11 For I know the thoughts that I think toward you, saith the LORD, thoughts of peace, and not of evil, to give you an expected end.

Prayer

- Our Father in Heaven, **we come into** Your **Most Holy presence to thank** You **for** Your **thoughts concerning Nigeria and us Nigerians.**

- **May it please** You, **O LORD our God, to establish** Your **thoughts concerning us and our nation, Nigeria, in the mighty name of** Jesus, **Amen. May this righteous Nigeria become a reality now, in the mighty name of** Jesus. **Amen.**

- **As kings and priests unto You, our God, we uproot and dislodge every obstacle of men and devils to the emergence of this righteous Nigeria, in the mighty name of** Jesus **we decree, Amen.**

- By the anointing of the Holy Spirit **upon us from** Your **presence, now, we call forth: A righteous Nigeria be loosed and come forth now, in the mighty name of** Jesus. **Amen.**

- **May it please** You, our Father, **to release** Your **ministering and actualizing angels to orchestrate this transformation from a corrupt Nigeria to a righteous Nigeria, in the all-conquering name of** Jesus **we ask. Amen.**

- **And now, we receive this righteous Nigeria from** God our Father, **in** Jesus' **mighty name, Amen. Thank** You, **our precious** Father, **for the realization of this righteous Nigeria. It is in the awesome name of** Jesus Christ **we have prayed. Amen and Amen.**

- **And now let one million voices rise to heaven every day, calling forth this Righteous Nigeria of prophecy, and the Finger of God Almighty will actualize it for us, in the name of** Jesus. **Amen**

Glory Alleluia!

The things that are visible (a Righteous Nigeria) are coming from things that are not visible (Prayer Decrees and the Finger of Almighty God).

KINGS AND PRIESTS UNTO GOD: UNDERSTANDING THE PRACTICE OF SPIRITUAL GOVERNANCE

Prepare to embark on a transformative journey within the pages of "Kings and Priests unto God." In this compelling work by Okey Onuzo, you'll unearth the extraordinary power of the righteous to govern and decree on Earth, aligning it with the divine will of God.

Unveiling the secrets of empowerment and the incredible potency of the anointing, this book shatters the chains that bind humanity to the devil's influence. No longer will you see Christians as weak, for within these chapters, you'll discover you are abundantly resourced by heaven itself to reign supreme on Earth.

Equip yourself with the knowledge and revelation that will forever change your perspective on your spiritual inheritance. "Kings and Priests" is your key to a life of authority and purpose. Don't miss this exhilarating release!

Printed in Great Britain
by Amazon

44002927R00086